Elizabeth Ann Seton

Saints by Our Side

Elizabeth Ann Seton

By Anne Merwin

Pauline
BOOKS & MEDIA
Boston

Library of Congress Cataloging-in-Publication Data

Merwin, Anne.
  Elizabeth Ann Seton / Anne Merwin.
    pages cm
  Includes bibliographical references.
  ISBN 978-0-8198-2380-9—ISBN 0-8198-2380-5
  1. Seton, Elizabeth Ann, Saint, 1774–1821. 2. Christian saints—United States—Biography. I. Title.
  BX4700.S4M47 2014
  271'.9102—dc23
  [B]

2014004071

The Scripture quotations contained herein are from the *New Revised Standard Version Bible: Catholic Edition,* copyright © 1989, 1993, Division of Christian Education of the National Council of the Churches of Christ in the United States of America. Used by permission. All rights reserved.

Excerpts from the English translation of the *Catechism of the Catholic Church* for use in the United States of America, copyright © 1994, United States Catholic Conference, Inc.—Libreria Editrice Vaticana. Used with permission.

Excerpts from *Elizabeth Bayley Seton Collected Writings,* 3 vols. (New York: New City Press, 2000–2006) copyright © Sisters of Charity Federation. Used with permission.

Excerpts from Rev. John David to Elizabeth Seton, Baltimore, 28 December 1809, Archives of Mount Saint Vincent (AMSV) 115, 1, 18. Courtesy: Archives Sisters of Charity of New York.

Excerpts from *Numerous Choirs, Volume I: The Seton Years, 1774–1821,* and the Archives Province of St. Louise (APSL) 1-3-3-4 #119, from Cecilia O'Conway, Christmas 1818. Courtesy: Daughters of Charity Province of St. Louise Archives, Emmitsburg, Maryland.

Excerpts from the *Canonization of Elisabeth Ann Seton, Homily of the Holy Father Paul VI,* September 14, 1975, copyright © Libreria Editrice Vaticana. Used with permission.

Excerpts from the Navy Medal Pamphlet, *Commemorating Elizabeth Ann Seton, 1774–1821, Sainted Mother of Two U.S. Navy Sons,* copyright © National Shrine of Saint Elizabeth Anne Seton, Emmitsburg, Maryland.

Cover design by Rosana Usselmann

Cover background photo: © istockphoto.com/ ver0nicka

Published by Pauline Books & Media, 50 Saint Pauls Avenue, Boston, MA 02130–3491

Printed in the U.S.A.

www.pauline.org

Pauline Books & Media is the publishing house of the Daughters of St. Paul, an international congregation of women religious serving the Church with the communications media.

1 2 3 4 5 6 7 8 9   19 18 17 16 15

"The Lord looks on the heart."
—1 SAMUEL 16:7

"God loves a cheerful giver."
—2 CORINTHIANS 9:7

"Think of him, love him, and look to him,
and never mind the rest—all will be well—
the Lord will direct."
—SAINT ELIZABETH ANN SETON[1]

"Perseverance and spirit have done wonders in all ages."
—GENERAL GEORGE WASHINGTON[2]

· · · · · · · · · · ·

Contents

· · · · · · · · · · · ·

My Personal Connection to Saint Elizabeth Ann Seton

"Faithful friends are a sturdy shelter: whoever finds one has found a treasure." (Sir 6:14)

I met Saint Elizabeth Ann Seton because of my husband. One weekend in the early 1990s, he suggested that we visit her house in Baltimore. He told me I had a great deal in common with her. I reluctantly agreed to put our active young sons in the car and go to a museum, where I would have to prevent them from running through the exhibits. When I arrived and walked through the front door of the Mother Seton House, I felt a peace that engulfed my mind, my body, and my soul. I knew I belonged there. From that day on, I have tried to learn as much as possible about Saint Elizabeth Ann Seton. What I did not realize was how much she would teach me about my own life through her example.

———•◆•———

We are all part of God's family through the communion of saints. My relationship with Elizabeth has another, earthly dimension, however, because I am related to her sister-in-law, Mary Hoffman Seton. I have other things in common with Elizabeth. She and I were both Episcopalians from New York City who converted to Catholicism while we cared for our young children. Her maternal grandfather was a Protestant clergyman, as was my maternal great-great-grandfather. Religion was ingrained in our families. Brought up to be debutantes, we went to private schools for girls and studied music. We both married men from New York who changed the direction of our lives. Circumstances concerning our husbands led us to Catholicism and to Baltimore at the age of thirty-three. Elizabeth found her mission in life while living at her house on Paca Street, and at that same house I discovered joy in promoting her legacy.

The other similar circumstances in our lives are too numerous to list here. They helped me understand Elizabeth's story. I never planned these events; they just happened. In retrospect, my connections to Elizabeth gradually and gently unfolded like a sunrise at dawn. Divine education teaches through revelation. My personal connections to Elizabeth can be best understood in light of a short overview of her life.

———•◆•———

It is not possible to speak of the spirit of Elizabeth without joining it to the spirit of her land, the new nation, for she came from its soil, breathed its air, and walked its streets. She dreamed its dreams, captured its vision, and lived the meaning of its pioneering experience.[1]

Elizabeth was brought up during the tumultuous times of the American Revolution. She was born in the area of New York City in 1774 into a wealthy, aristocratic, and Episcopalian family. Her parents were preoccupied with the war and their expanding family while Elizabeth was growing up. Elizabeth's faith in God comforted her and became a source of strength.

In 1789, George Washington was sworn in as the first President of the United States at New York City's Federal Hall on Wall Street. The same year, Bishop John Carroll became the head of the nation's first Catholic Diocese in Baltimore. Elizabeth would convert to Catholicism; and her later association with Bishop Carroll gave her the opportunity for leadership in the formative years of the Catholic Church in America. The year 1789 was a year of spiritual growth and formation for the teen-aged Elizabeth. She discovered that God, who revealed himself to her in nature, was also her Father.

In 1794, Elizabeth married William Magee Seton, of the prominent Seton mercantile family. She bore five children in the next eight years. Then tragedy struck several times in quick succession. Elizabeth courageously faced the failure of her husband's business and his painful death from tuberculosis. Inspired by her stay in Catholic Italy at the time of her husband's death, Elizabeth returned to New York in 1804 only to face struggle once again. She decided to give up her social standing, withstood the rejection of family members (which included my relative, Mary Seton), and, to the horror of New York society, she converted to Catholicism. This penniless widow with five children persisted while making such a bold move. And it got the attention of Baltimore's Bishop John Carroll.

In 1808, John Carroll approved the invitation of Reverend Louis William Valentine Dubourg, the President of Saint Mary's College in Baltimore, to have Elizabeth start a Catholic school for girls on its grounds. With extraordinary perseverance and hard work, she managed to bring up her own five children while she accomplished pioneering work for the Catholic school system and establishing the first order of Catholic sisters in the United States. From their formation days in Baltimore and Emmitsburg, Maryland, her Sisters and Daughters of Charity would travel across the United States and around the globe to establish new foundations. On September 14, 1975, the world celebrated the canonization of Elizabeth Ann Seton, the first native-born saint of the United States.

Elizabeth's life and work teach us how to put faith into action. She responded to the needs of each day and to the events of her time. She answered the call of Christ with a grateful and willing heart. She accepted God's will and moved forward.

———•◆•———

Three memorable experiences solidified both my connection with Elizabeth and my commitment to her legacy. I can label these experiences human, historic, and holy.

Elizabeth's humanity became evident to me in the winter of 2000. In January, one of my children hit a tree hard while sledding at dusk. While I waited in the hospital's emergency room for my son to return from getting x-rays, I prayed for Saint Elizabeth Ann Seton's intercession and promptly fell asleep. It was the last thing I wanted to do, because I intended to pray for a positive outcome the entire time he was having the x-rays. Upon waking, I immediately learned that my son suffered much bruising, but he did not break any bones. He would be fine, but I needed to recover. The only sleep I got that night was when my son was in the x-ray department.

In retrospect, not only were my prayers for my son answered, but I also got a few minutes of rest, which I needed for the following day.

When we left the hospital early the next morning, I realized the deeper significance of the nap. When I fell asleep, I lost control of my prayers. My agenda to pray continuously during the x-rays peacefully slipped into God's gentle, correcting hands. I believed that God, helped by the loving intercession of a maternal friend in heaven for an anxious mother on earth, knew what I really needed. I learned that I could finally trust God to set my agenda. In gratitude, I decided to commit as much of my life as possible to promoting the legacy of Saint Elizabeth Ann Seton.

Historic saintly connections can seem like coincidences. People have told me that they became interested in Elizabeth because her saint's day happened to be their birthdays or anniversaries. Others said that, like Elizabeth, they had five children or that they were one of five. These shared circumstances are factual magnets that draw people to Elizabeth and anchors that keep them interested in her. They also can become holy, life-changing, faith-filled experiences. The first time I heard Elizabeth's story at her house in Baltimore, I reacted by thinking: *An Episcopalian woman married in Lower Manhattan who converted to Catholicism and moved to Baltimore . . . wow, I did that, too!* I was hooked and had to learn more.

I read that Elizabeth had worshiped at Saint Paul's Episcopal Church in New York and had felt drawn by the nearby Catholic church of Saint Peter during her decision to convert to Catholicism. I had spent many lunch hours praying in Episcopal churches in mid-town Manhattan wondering why I felt something missing, why I was not quite connecting. When I stepped into the nearby Saint Patrick's Cathedral, I knew I had found the comfort of the missing link. It was the presence of the Blessed Sacrament, although I did not understand what that meant at the time. Now I feel most closely connected to Elizabeth in prayer that takes place in the presence of the Blessed Sacrament, either privately or at Mass.

Finally there are the holy experiences that seem to include all dimensions of life. In the spring of 2006, almost exactly 200 years after Elizabeth's confirmation at Saint Peter's Catholic Church in New York by Baltimore's Bishop John Carroll, I visited the Parrocchia Madre Seton in Livorno, Italy (the first church in Europe named for Mother Seton). In Livorno, Elizabeth would become interested in the Catholic faith while staying with the Filicchi family after her husband's death. In the garden of this church named after Mother Seton, her statue stands most appropriately between the graves of her husband, William, and their mutual Catholic friend Antonio Filicchi. She holds a rosary in one hand and a book in the other. The book reminded me of my Protestant days when I began to study the Bible, and the Rosary represented my Catholic faith and prayers to Mary, the Queen of All Saints.

The juxtaposition of the graves was deeply moving. The friendship of William Seton and Antonio Filicchi was honored in a way that revealed the beauty of God's love in his plan for Elizabeth's life. Through these men, Elizabeth's life as wife and mother became that of widow, convert, and foundress. The unity of the American and Italian men reflected the universality of the Church. In nature's peaceful setting, history met eternity in the sanctity of Elizabeth. And through the death and resurrection of Christ, we all have hope for a blessed eternity. In the silence of that garden, in the presence of earthly and heavenly friends, in a country where I could not understand the language, I finally understood the meaning of the Communion of Saints.

What does Elizabeth mean to me?

She has enlightened my life for the past twenty years. I have tried to visit the places in the world where her footsteps have left historical imprints. On a summer's day you can see me on the upper deck of the Governor's Island ferry in New York's harbor. Camera in hand, I click away at the approaching Manhattan skyline. For right in the center of that coastline is the site of Elizabeth's former home. In Baltimore, it was my great privilege and joy to show visitors her home and the chapel where she became Mother Seton. And as I approach Emmitsburg in my car during the different seasons of the year, I can see how Elizabeth must have felt this was truly God's country. I simply never get tired of retracing her timeless footsteps.

When I arrive at the National Shrine of Saint Elizabeth Ann Seton in Emmitsburg, I slip into the old cemetery to visit the graves of her two teenaged daughters and two beloved sisters-in-law. I ask for Elizabeth Seton's intercession for my family. Then I pray for her girls and soul sisters as well.

Elizabeth is like a jewel. The many beautiful facets in her legacy of love continue to sparkle. She trusted in God and thrived in the present. Yet she saw the present through the lens of eternity. She is a mentor and a heroic model of holiness. Best of all, she is a friend who is always available. I think of the words in Proverbs, "Many women have done excellently, but you surpass them all" (Prov 31:29).

In the following pages, I have attempted to show how God motivated Elizabeth's thoughts and actions.[2] My hope is the example of her life, one of divine education, can reveal the love and mission God has for your life. The reflections and questions at the end of the book are designed for that purpose.

If you feel particularly drawn to Elizabeth, I hope this book will help you understand why. In *A Simple Life*, Kathryn Hermes, FSP, beautifully describes the connection to a saint.

> It is a blessed moment when one discovers a kindred spirit among the saints. When this happens, it often becomes apparent that the spiritual friendship had been developing quietly and patiently throughout life, waiting for the moment when it would blossom into a kinship of the soul.[3]

All saints have demonstrated extraordinary virtues, especially charity. So even if you have a different vocation from

Elizabeth's, it is still possible to imitate the purpose and motivation of her life. She loved God with her whole heart, mind, and soul. She also loved her neighbor. Through God's timeless love, the years melt away. Therefore, her neighbor today includes you.

· · · · · · · · · · · ·

Chapter One

Spiritual Seeds and Formation

"Look up at the blue Heavens and love Him!" [1]

As you approach the tip of lower Manhattan aboard the deck of a slow-moving ferry, the tall, gleaming glass buildings of State and Water Streets beckon. From this majestic, thin tip of the island, every linear structure reaches for its place in the spacious blue skies. But what is the tiny brick building front and center, nestled between two skyscrapers? More importantly, how can it justify the land it occupies in both the continuously evolving New York skyline and one of the most valuable real estate markets in the world? This three-story Georgian style house is associated with the legacy of Saint Elizabeth Ann Seton, the first native-born Catholic saint of the United States. Today, it is both a parish church and a shrine to Saint Elizabeth Ann Seton. Her journey began in New York City in 1774, but now her legacy is worldwide, eternal, and accessible to all. Just as this site where she lived over two hundred years ago has endured to become a church that welcomes visitors from around the globe, her story still invites everyone to share in its relevance today.

———•◆•———

Elizabeth Ann Bayley was born in the area of New York City on August 28, 1774, the feast of Saint Augustine. In November 1773, almost nine months before her birth, a British ship loaded with tea docked in Boston Harbor. Unwilling to pay the import tax to Britain, colonists failed to convince the proper authorities to have the ship return to England. A few people dressed up as Native American warriors and threw the cargo of tea overboard. Later known as the Boston Tea Party, the event was a bold act of defiance and a stunning protest that helped spark the American Revolution.

The leaders of the American Revolution cared deeply for the freedom that liberates the soul. Although the fight to secure independence would add risk and pain to the immediate future of many colonists, the vision of liberty fortified their ability to persevere.

As a child of the American Revolution, Elizabeth possessed the same qualities its leaders had: faith, foresight, and fortitude. Instead of using guns and swords to plow ahead, she used a gentle combination of prayer and action to skillfully outmaneuver the conventions and prejudices of her day. Rather than igniting a cannon's blast, Elizabeth quietly lit the flame of innovation one candle at a time, until the warmth and light caught on.

Elizabeth's childhood was intertwined with American history. One month after her birth in 1774, delegates from twelve of the thirteen original colonies, prompted by the Boston Tea Party, met as the First Continental Congress. The British prepared for a struggle. In 1775, Paul Revere warned the colonists in Massachusetts of the British army's advance, and the American Revolutionary War began.

By Elizabeth's first birthday, over three quarters of New York City's residents had fled due to the threat of war with Great Britain.[2] Elizabeth and her family probably moved to the comparative safety of Staten Island, staying with her maternal grandparents, the Reverend Richard and Mrs. Mary Bayeux Charlton.

Just before her second birthday, the Battle of Long Island started. The British were well prepared to fight and dominate by sea and by land. A month later, the Great Fire of 1776 devastated about one fourth of New York City, including her Uncle William Bayley's store and Trinity Church on Wall Street, which might have contained Elizabeth's baptismal records (they have not yet been found). The Declaration of Independence of 1776 had a backlash. Richard Bayley, Elizabeth's father, experienced the consequences first hand. As an army surgeon based in Newport, Rhode Island, during the beginning of the war,[3] he was thoroughly acquainted with the fear and acute brutality of war. Later, as the first Public Health Commissioner of New York City, Dr. Bayley also dealt with the war's aftermath of poverty, destruction, and disease. In 1777, he returned to his ailing wife and young family in New York.

—•—

The Bayleys were a prominent family of French and English descent. Elizabeth was the second of three daughters born to Dr. Richard and Catherine Charlton Bayley. During Elizabeth's early childhood, her mother and younger sister died. Elizabeth coped with their deaths by focusing her thoughts on heaven. By looking up into the distant sky, her mind could reach out to a place where her mother and sister now existed in the fullness of God's love. In her day, the urban sky was still mysterious and peaceful. If it became cloudy, unpredictable, and stormy, it still held hope for change. Just as the earth depends on the sky for light, air, and water, the little, lonely Elizabeth instinctively looked up to God for sustenance. He in turn nurtured her soul.

In June 1778, Richard Bayley married Charlotte Amelia Barclay, a member of the prominent Roosevelt family. The new Mrs. Bayley would have six children over the next eight years.[4] But she found time to teach Elizabeth to pray Psalm 23, "The Lord is my Shepherd," which remained her favorite psalm throughout her life. The image of the Good Shepherd comforted her.

During this time period, women were often left at home to run farms and businesses while the men were at sea or war. Dr. Bayley was a successful and well-known teacher of anatomy at King's College (now Columbia University), then located in Lower Manhattan. His medical studies and research required him to be in England for months at a time. He understood the need for education to prepare both men and women for self-sufficiency in a tumultuous, young country. Dr. Bayley sent Elizabeth to a private girls' school where she received a profit-able education.

As more children were born to Dr. Bayley and his second wife, Elizabeth was often sent to her Uncle Bayley's house* on the unspoiled, sparkling blue shores of Long Island Sound near New Rochelle. She spent many hours alone, walking in the leafy woods inhabited by the birds and animals. Along the sandy beaches and marshy coves, she listened to the sounds of the geese and seagulls that filled the air. There she felt close to God. The wind was his breath, the skies his domain, and the tiny wild flowers the artwork of his creation. One day in the spring of 1789, during her father's absence abroad, the teenaged Elizabeth felt the presence of God in nature fill the painful parental void in her life. His love filled her heart as her eyes were drawn toward a family of chestnut trees. The beauty of nature took hold of her senses, and her soul soared with wonder. She realized and rejoiced that God was her Father and wrote that she "then layed still to enjoy the Heavenly Peace that came over my Soul; and I am sure in the two hours so enjoyed grew ten years in my spiritual life."[5] Just as teenagers throughout the centuries begin to reach out to peers and friends for support and companionship as they mature, Elizabeth's receptive heart found both her mentor and the recipient for her love in God.

———•◆•———

---

* Today, the Bayley house is near the border of Pelham and New Rochelle in New York. It is privately owned and visible from the street. The nearby Glen Island Park in New Rochelle provides a good view of Long Island Sound. It is easy to picture the teenaged Elizabeth here, especially on the leafy shore road.

Elizabeth had always felt the presence of God in her young life, but now she understood the nature of this connection and recognized its meaning. God was both her Creator and her parent. According to the *Catechism of the Catholic Church*, "He [God] ... transcends human fatherhood and motherhood ... no one is father as God is Father" (*CCC*, no. 239). And "If my father and my mother forsake me, the LORD will take me up" (Ps 27:10).

Of course Elizabeth's parents did not intentionally forsake her. Her mother had died, and her father's career required him to be absent. Her stepmother had young children who required constant attention. But when a heart such as Elizabeth's is vulnerable, it requires tender care. God provided the warmth and love she needed.

Around the age of eighteen, Elizabeth entered the culturally sophisticated world of wealthy New York society. Upper-class girls of her time were exposed to the social graces of polite conversation, manners, and diplomacy. Tiny (just under five feet) and slim, Elizabeth had a lovely, open face, large brown eyes, and long, wavy brown hair. From all accounts of her beauty, she must have been the type of woman who could wear any style with ease. A talented musician, she loved to dance so much that she kept her dancing slippers all her life. At her National Shrine in Emmitsburg, Maryland, you can see her delicate, white-silk dancing shoes with an "S" on the toe area. With any debutante, a gentle and sparkling personality adds bounce to a dance step. Whether Elizabeth twirled across the ballrooms of eighteenth-century New York or later walked the dirt roads of rural Maryland as an American Catholic pioneer, God always led her in the dance, and she graciously followed.

—•◆•—

Even as a teenager, Elizabeth was easy to understand because her soul was uncluttered. She was honest, imaginative, poetic, and emotional. She knew how to stand her ground. She gave what she could and was grateful for what she received. Her generous heart not only served others but also respected and forgave them. Of course she had her faults; she wrote about her sins and weaknesses. She asked for God's forgiveness, that he weed and prune her soul so that she could see his purpose for her daily life. Thus she wished to know herself in order to recognize her full potential in the service of God. Fortified with self-knowledge, she faced the world ready to give to others what God had given her. She desired his approval more than the approval of the people around her.

Through the power of the Holy Spirit, God gave her the ability she needed to serve him. Her qualities are similar to the fruit of the Holy Spirit: "The fruit of the Spirit is love, joy, peace, patience, kindness, generosity, faithfulness, gentleness, and self-control" (Gal 5:22–23).

Her life incorporated the gifts of the Holy Spirit as well. They are described in the Book of Isaiah.

> The spirit of the LORD shall rest on him, the spirit of wisdom and understanding, the spirit of counsel and might, the spirit of knowledge and the fear of the LORD. His delight shall be in the fear of the Lord. He shall not judge by what his eyes see, or decide by what his ears hear. (Isa 11:2–3)

Elizabeth's joy came from living Christ's words, "I give you a new commandment, that you love one another. Just as I have loved you, you also should love one another" (Jn 13:34). She

loved others through charity. If people were difficult, she persevered and sacrificed, knowing that her reward was God's peace
and joy.[6]

CHAPTER TWO

· · · · · · · · · · · ·

Marriage and Motherhood

*"My precious children stick to me like little Burrs . . . the
moment I shake one off one side another clings in the opposite,
nor can I write one word without some sweet interrup-
tion . . ."*[1]

In 1794, Elizabeth married William Magee Seton, a member
of a distinguished Scottish family. She was nineteen, and he
was twenty-six. William's ancestor, Mary Seton, was a lady-in-
waiting to Mary Queen of Scots. His father, William, was the
first Treasurer of the Bank of New York. Alexander Hamilton, an
acquaintance and neighbor of Elizabeth's, served on the Board of
Directors of this bank.[2] William Magee Seton's mother, Rebecca
Curson Seton, died during his youth, just as Elizabeth's mother
had. His father remarried Anna-Maria Curson, Rebecca's sister,
and had several more children.

The elder Seton was a devoted family man. He always thought about the welfare of others.[3] Elizabeth admired him. Both her father and father-in-law provided Elizabeth with strong models of charity and self-sacrifice in the service of others. William senior also ran the family's commercial shipping firm: Seton, Maitland, and Company. As part of his training for the shipping business, William Magee Seton spent time in Europe before his marriage, visiting ports in Spain and Italy. William traveled to Livorno, Italy, where his father's Italian friends, the Filicchis, lived.[4] Antonio and Filippo Filicchi became close friends with William and, later, with Elizabeth. The friendship of these families has endured to this day in the legacy of Elizabeth's sanctity.

Much like today, New York in the 1790s had basically three social classes: the wealthy and powerful social elite, the middle class workers who were often shopkeepers or government employees, and the lower class laborers or servants.[5] Poorer immigrants, as well as distinguished visitors from overseas, such as British and French diplomats, also lived in the city.

As members of the upper class, the young Setons were married at home, considered fashionable at the time, and even more socially exciting if the bishop performed the ceremony.[6] It is thought that Elizabeth was married at the home of her older sister, Mary Post. Mary was married to Dr. Wright Post, a prominent physician and colleague of Elizabeth's father. Bishop Samuel Provoost, the Bishop of New York City who had presided over George Washington's inaugural prayer service in 1789, conducted the Setons' marriage ceremony.[7]

Elizabeth and William were exposed to an international society in New York. Upper class women were trained to entertain foreign diplomats and to converse in French, which was the language of the European aristocracy. The Seton's international mercantile firm imported fine goods from Europe and North America.

As the capital, New York City was at the summit of fashion and culture. Women were conscious of how they looked and acted. They were more independent-minded than their British contemporaries. In the words of an Englishman writing about American women in the 1790s: "New York is the gayest place in America. . . . The ladies, however, are not solely employed in attention to dress; there are many who are studious to add to [their] brilliant external accomplishments."[8] Elizabeth was one of these women. She and her husband would help to host George Washington's sixty-fifth birthday ball.

At first the young Setons lived with William's father on Stone Street in Lower Manhattan. Today part of this cobblestone street is filled with tables of outdoor diners who relish the ability to relax, catch a bit of sun, and eat and drink al fresco in the high pressured atmosphere of the Financial District. The young married couple then moved into their own house at 27 Wall Street,* where Elizabeth still focused her thoughts on heaven, "my own home at 20—the world—that and heaven too, quite impossible!"[9]

---

* Elizabeth's house at 27 Wall Street does not exist today. The location is diagonally across the street from the former New York Stock Exchange, known now as the NYSE Euronext, and across Wall Street from Federal Hall. The knowledge that Elizabeth lived here and worshiped in nearby Trinity Church gives a spiritual dimension to this corner of the United States.

A happy couple, Elizabeth and William were blessed with five children in their first eight years together. Elizabeth's love for her children—Anna Maria, William, Richard Bayley, Catherine Charlton, and Rebecca Mary—is best described in her words to her son, William, in 1817:

> If a Mother's love could be a fortune to you, you would be rich indeed. Alas, it is poor coin in this world, but be assured it will have its interest in heaven where it solicits, I may truly say, day and night, for every blessing on you.[10]

Elizabeth had her share of maternal trials and challenges. To mothers anywhere and at any time, her comforting words speak from experience, "Our God alone knows a Mother's heart, and he will pity us."[11] She also cautioned losing one's peace of mind by doing too much: "you will help others more by the peace and tranquility of your heart than by any eagerness or care you can bestow on them"[12] In other words, "nothing can be more pressing than the necessity for your peace before God."[13]

———•◆•———

In the summer of 1798, William's father died. Elizabeth was weak from the birth of her third child, Richard Seton. She was also coping with her oldest daughter, Anna, who had an "ungovernable temper."[14] After his father's death, William not only inherited the responsibilities of the family firm, but also the staggering duty of bringing up his seven younger brothers and sisters. Much of that work fell to Elizabeth.

That same year, the Seton shipping firm suffered many losses. Storms, pirates, and English and French warships prevented

William from fulfilling his contracts. Elizabeth persevered through round-the-clock problems with a courageous spirit worthy of the saint she would become. She never seemed angry with the circumstances that put the family in such a desperate state. Instead, she tried to keep both the business and William's spirits from collapsing. She lived her marriage vows, "for better for worse, for richer for poorer, in sickness and in health."[15] Elizabeth described her determination this way: "Hope must go on with us, for it will not do for hearts and fortunes to sink together."[16]

When it became obvious that William's business would not recover from its losses, Elizabeth wisely accepted what she could not change. To her friend Julia Scott, she wrote:

> I will tell you the plain truth, that my habits both of Soul and Body are changed—that I feel all the habits of society and connections of this life have taken a new form and are only interesting or endearing as they point the view to the next.[17]

She was beginning to exchange her past and present connections in this world for assurance in the next.

Change can be frightening, but the reluctant spirit is reassured with these words, "Jesus can never give you a task above your courage, strength, or ability."[18] When the business situation became critical, William needed his wife more than ever. Tuberculosis had plagued him for years, and the disease and added stress of his declining business began to take their toll. Elizabeth sought comfort in her religion. She exemplified the supporting wife who tries to be a rock of faith in the face of adversity, uncertainty, and humiliation. Each day she radiated hope in an ocean of despair, and she conveyed a peace that passes all understanding.

> How he (William) will get through it I know not, and it is
> well for me I have a perfect reliance on Superior Providence,
> or my spirits would be unequal to the task of supporting his.[19]

In 1799, the financial state of William's business turned desperate. Elizabeth helped out by going over the accounting books in whatever free time she could find.

Reflecting on the previous year, she wrote, "[M]y poor William has kept me constantly employed in copying his letters and assisting him to arrange his Papers for he has no friend or confidant now on Earth but his little wife."[20] But the damage could not be reversed. It became clear that William could not support his family and also his stepbrothers and stepsisters. Toward the end of 1800, William faced debtor's prison. Elizabeth wrote, "the House [Seton, Maitland, and Company] is to be declared Bankrupt . . . or Seton must go to Prison."[21] The day after Christmas she wrote that she had "given up my list to the Commissioners of Bankruptcy of all we possess, even to our and the children's clothing. . . ."[22] It looked as if things couldn't get any worse, but they did. In the meantime, Elizabeth's grateful and generous heart reached out to others in need.

———•◆•———

Life often turns out differently from what we expect. In the early 1800s in New York, a woman's life was bound to her family's fate. If circumstances deteriorated, a wife and mother had few opportunities to take charge and turn things around. When men were at war or absent, women did their best to keep their homes, farms, and even businesses functioning. When the men were disabled or died, the women and children, who did not have a network of family, friends, or other women to help them, became destitute. If a man lost his money or if his business failed, a family would follow him to debtors' prison. The government did not have organized programs such as welfare to relieve a family's suffering. Charity was mostly provided by religious institutions.

Elizabeth witnessed the plight of the poor and looked on them with compassion and empathy. She saw in them an opportunity to help. Her father, Dr. Bayley, attended the poor and sick immigrants who arrived at the docks of New York with hopes of starting a new life in America. Some of those people never had a chance to act upon their hopes and realize their dreams.

Although her husband was losing his money and health, her family still had loyal friends and relatives who could possibly assist them. However, she knew about widows and orphans less fortunate than herself who struggled to survive day to day. She understood that the only way God could answer their pleas and needs was to send laborers into their presence. Elizabeth heard the cry of the poor and responded by using her leadership and organizational talents. While her father cared for the medical needs of the poor, she joined a group of women who provided physical necessities, a listening ear, and hope in suffering. Her faith in God and love for others gave her ample motivation to find time in her busy life to do his work.

In the late 1790s, Elizabeth met with friends to form the Society for the Relief of Poor Widows with Small Children, which was informally known as the Protestant Sisters of Charity. She became the Treasurer of the Society,[23] which raised money for widows and organized visits to the poor. This Society became known as the first charitable organization United States managed by women.

———•◆•———

In 1801, Elizabeth's beloved father, Dr. Richard Bayley, died from yellow fever that he contracted from treating immigrants in the quarantine station. Elizabeth was with him during his last days. Around that time, she relied more on God to carry her through her struggles. She greatly admired the Episcopal minister, Reverend John Henry Hobart of Trinity Church on Wall Street. A skilled orator, Hobart inspired Elizabeth's interest in religion. He noticed her piety,[24] and a mutual spiritual respect was born.

After her father's death, the Seton family moved to 8 State Street on the Battery. In August 1802, Elizabeth's youngest child, Rebecca, was born in this house. It would be the last home that Elizabeth and William shared—though not for long.

In 1803, William's tuberculosis overwhelmed him. In a desperate attempt to save or at least prolong her husband's life, Elizabeth and William decided to travel to the warmer climate of Livorno, Italy. They planned to stay with the Setons' friends, the Filicchis, and would take with them their oldest daughter, Anna. Relatives and friends would care for the four younger children she left behind. It was a bold act of devotion and courage. The seas were not safe, Elizabeth had just weaned a sick baby, and her friends cautioned that attempting such a voyage would be "madness."[25] But Elizabeth replied, "you know that I go fearless."[26] For "all is well and resting on the mercy of God."[27]

It is also possible that Elizabeth wished to remove her husband from the pressure of his business failure. In 1803, William was beginning to draw nearer to God. Leaving New York behind gave Elizabeth more freedom and time to concentrate on the spiritual dimension of her marriage and on the good of William's soul. Or perhaps she hoped God would intervene in some way. "My Seton's decline is so rapid that there can be no hope of his recovery in the view of MORTAL HOPES."[28] Whatever her reasons, for the Setons to leave for Italy, they certainly outweighed the advantages of staying in their present situation. It seemed more logical to move forward into the unknown.

In October 1803, Elizabeth, William, and Anna would sail out of New York harbor on the *Shepherdess* to Italy. This seven week voyage would change the course of their lives.

Elizabeth embraced these changing circumstances with honesty and faith. In her words, "If it succeeds, I bless God, if . . . [it] does not succeed, I bless God, because then it will be right that it should not succeed."[29] By assessing her efforts in this way, she learned from her experiences and moved on. Failure did not weigh her down, because she offered it right back up to God. Her example gives us hope that what appears to go wrong in our lives can be just what we need to help us move on. Risks become opportunities in disguise. She advised others to "resign the present and future to Him who is the Author and conductor of both . . ."[30]

At times she looked back on the more pleasant, easier days of her early marriage. In hindsight, she realized that she did not fully appreciate what she had. With a sad but determined heart, she wrote:

> Who can help looking back on . . . past pleasures without
> sorrow. . . . I could cry like a child at the thought of them, but
> resolved to brave the future. I turn over the Page with rapid-
> ity, and looking towards Heaven there fix my aim—there is
> no change.[31]

The frequency and degree of change in Elizabeth's life were extraordinary, and they help people to connect with her, because they can identify with her experiences. Throughout her life, she grew with the history of the country. She knew the personal consequences of living in a military family, first as a daughter of an army surgeon during the Revolutionary War and then as a navy mother. She was rich and privileged, impoverished and scorned, humiliated and respected. As a Protestant laywoman or a Catholic sister, Elizabeth's faith stood out. She was an educator, foundress, and leader of a religious community. She remained devoted to her family as a daughter, sister, sister-in-law, wife, mother, widow, and single mother who knew the anguish of burying a husband and two teenaged daughters.

Whether serving in the bustling cities of New York and Baltimore or in the comparatively primitive, pastoral setting of Emmitsburg, she persevered through change and triumphed against the odds. Elizabeth coped with the twists and turns of daily life by placing them into the transforming hands of God. Instead of succumbing to despair, Elizabeth lived these words of Proverbs 3:5–6: "Trust in the LORD with all your heart, and do not rely on your own insight. In all your ways acknowledge him, and he will make straight your paths." While Elizabeth coped with change, she was even able to help form the widows' society to assist other women in worse circumstances.

She would eventually become one of those destitute widows. But her story does not end there. God did not abandon her. If he closed the door of her married life with her husband's death, he also opened a new one. Elizabeth's introduction to the Catholic faith in Italy would guide her along new paths during her desperate days of widowhood in New York and for the remainder of her life.

· · · · · · · · · · · ·

CHAPTER THREE

Livorno: Tragedy Transformed

"I have been in a sea of troubles . . . but the guiding star is always bright, and the master of the storm always in view." [1]

In the fall of 1803, Elizabeth, William, and Anna Seton said goodbye to their family in New York and boarded their ship to Italy. They sailed out of their past into the unchartered seas of life. The trip to Italy would bring both promise and pain.

The sea voyage provided refreshing breezes for William's health and inspiring sunsets for Elizabeth's imagination, but it also placed them in the midst of driving rains, crashing waves, and unrelenting winds from which they could not escape. Elizabeth's faith kept her on a steady course to the future.

As Elizabeth passed the halfway mark in her trip to Livorno, she reflected on the tranquility of her soul: ". . . confiding Hope and consoling Peace have attended my way thro' storms and dangers that must have terrified a Soul whose Rock is not Christ."[2] A few days later the ship passed through the Bay of Gibraltar between the continents of Europe and Africa. During this passage she dreamt she "was climbing with great difficulty a Mountain of immense height and blackness" when she heard a voice say, "Never mind take courage there is a beautiful green hill on the other side—and on it an angel waits for you."[3]

From a distance, the Rock of Gibraltar may look intimidating. But as you approach the rock, the shore comes into focus and you can begin to recognize people, hear the noises of the harbor, and smell the vegetation. Elizabeth faced her daily challenges with this same perspective. The closer we draw to God in faith, the more surmountable obstacles become. Challenges and suffering take on a fresh, outward-reaching meaning because God ". . . consoles us in all our affliction, so that we may be able to console those who are in any affliction with the consolation with which we ourselves are consoled by God" (2 Cor 1:4).

God was Elizabeth's rock, her comfort, and her hope. He helped release her from the burdens of fear, self-doubt, and worry that accompany suffering. She accepted hardships and responsibility without blaming people or events for her problems. Elizabeth responded to personal situations and to her time in history with the fullness of God's time. With God as her guide, she could safely navigate through the rough seas of life. "For the LORD is a great God, and a great King above all gods. In his hand are the depths of the earth; the heights of the mountains are his also. The sea is his, for he made it, and the dry land, which his hands have formed" (Ps 95:3–5).

—— ·◆· ——

After seven weeks at sea, the *Shepherdess* docked at the bustling, international port of Livorno in Tuscany. Livorno is known as "Little Venice" due to its beautiful, greenish-blue canals. The wall built 400 years ago to protect the city from invaders still stands today.

When the Setons arrived in November, the weather was perhaps milder than in New York, but it was not warm. The Italian authorities who greeted the ship presented a series of raw, chilling facts. Due to William's sickly constitution authorities feared the possibility of their carrying the yellow fever epidemic from New York. So the family of three would be quarantined off the docks of Livorno in a damp, primitive brick building known as the *lazaretto*. Not only was the yellow fever diagnosis frustrating and incorrect, but it also was painfully cruel for Elizabeth to hear. She had been at her father's bedside while he died from the yellow fever.

Elizabeth's reaction upon entering the dismal "prison" room of the *lazaretto*, which would be the Setons' home for an indefinite time, was to sink to her knees in the privacy of a small closet and burst into tears.[4] She was physically and mentally worn out, but she still had a job to do. After releasing her emotions, she emerged from the closet ready to provide comfort and hope to her desperately ill and equally discouraged husband. It wasn't easy. In her words, "If I could forget my God one moment at these times I should go mad."[5]

The closet had a window overlooking the surrounding sea.[6] Salt from the waves covered the windowpanes and obscured much of the view. Back in the room, there was no relief from the noisy winds and icy drafts that seeped through the dank, brick walls. And there was no escape from the room itself. Elizabeth had to face a physical suffering similar to what we might endure today during an extended winter power outage.

—•—

It was an ironic twist of fate that, after surviving a perilous two-month journey across the Atlantic, the Setons' plans should be shipwrecked the moment their boat docked in Italy. William's illness had caused the family enough suffering, and they had looked forward to some respite in the comfortable accommodations provided by the Filicchis. However, another scenario loomed ahead that would stretch the limits of Elizabeth's mind, body, and soul. Elizabeth's account of the *lazaretto* is rich, spiritual writing on a bleak, empty, and isolated stage. In her mind, the isolation of the *lazaretto* was a blessing. It was indeed. By means of her journal, the journey of her soul and that of her husband's was clearly and slowly marked out, so that it became a microcosm of divine education.

If Elizabeth had been in New York during the final stages of William's illness, she would have had to deal with the time-consuming demands of her four younger children, the management of her depleted household, and the feelings of concerned relatives, not to mention the creditors. . . . In the *lazaretto*, her only responsibilities were the welfare of her husband and daughter. She was free to pray constantly and to record her feelings. "I find my present opportunity a Treasure—and my confinement of Body a liberty of Soul."[7] The strength of her faith was remarkable. Reading her account of how she faced her husband's losing battle with tuberculosis provides valiant examples of how to face struggle. Her soul gave warmth to the cold room, and her love of God throughout her trials provided hope.

The quarantine prevented Elizabeth from going to church. The Protestant minister, Reverend Hall, visited the *lazaretto*,[8] but it is unlikely that Elizabeth had the opportunity or privacy to obtain frequent spiritual support and direction through soul-searching conversations. However, she had always enjoyed being alone with God. Her personal relationship with God as her spiritual Father gave her what she needed to carry on and overcome.

Of course, at times, it was all too much.

> Consider my husband who left his all to seek a milder climate, confined in this place of high and damp walls exposed to cold and wind which penetrates to the very bones. . . . No little syrup . . . milk . . . bitter tea, and opium pills which he takes quietly as a duty without seeming even to hope, is all I can offer him from day to day. When . . . I can no longer look up with cheerfulness, I hide my head on the chair by his bedside and he thinks I am praying—and pray I do—for prayer is all my comfort, without which I should be of little service to him.[9]

Her prayers must have worked, because she also wrote: "He very often says this is the period of his life which, if he lives or dies, he will always consider as Blessed."[10]

William, in turn, inspired Elizabeth by his patience, forbearance, humility, and ability to endure his afflictions with grace.

> No sufferings, nor weakness nor distress . . . can prevent his following me daily in Prayer, portions of the Psalms, and generally large Portions of the Scriptures. . . .[11] I should bless and Praise my God for these days of retirement and

abstraction from the world, which have afforded leisure and opportunity for so blessed a work.[12]

On Christmas Day, just after their release from the *lazaretto*, Elizabeth wrote that she had poured some wine in a glass and then "we took the cup of Thanksgiving setting aside the sorrow of time, in the views of the joys of Eternity."[13] Elizabeth and William clearly accepted the present and looked forward to eternity for their future.

In the *lazaretto*, William was free to commit his life to Christ in an environment where the past did not matter and the only hope of the future was God. If he had stayed in New York, he would have died with friends and family nearby. In the *lazaretto*, William and Elizabeth were isolated when they prepared for his final journey home to God. Elizabeth positively influenced her husband's faith through the bond of her marriage. She was grief-stricken and naturally anxious at times, but not incapacitated or selfish. She had gratitude for the present and great hope for eternity. Elizabeth may not have saved William's physical life by going to Italy, but in the *lazaretto*, she and her husband worked together with God to assure the survival of his soul. They were blessed with joy.

> With God for our Portion, there is no Prison in high walls and bolts—no sorrow in the Soul . . . though beset with present cares and gloomy Prospects. For this freedom I can never be sufficiently thankful. . . .[14] Often when he (William) hears me repeat the Psalms of Triumph in God, and read St. Paul's faith in Christ with my Whole Soul, it so enlivens his Spirit that he also makes them his own, and all our sorrows are turned into joy.[15]

———•◆•———

When faced with unexpected trials, it is sometimes difficult to know whether to laugh or cry. Elizabeth did both. She led her family in singing hymns. Elizabeth also found comic relief in the *lazaretto*.

The *lazaretto* wasn't all bad. The Filicchis sent a servant to bring the Setons food and other provisions to make their accommodations more bearable. The kind, emotional *Capitano*, who oversaw the *lazaretto*, provided gifts of fruit and nuts from his own home.

The *lazaretto* room had a "brick floor, naked walls, and a jug of water."[16] Could the accommodations get any worse? Well, yes. The bone-chilling cold forced the mother and daughter to skip rope and hop on one foot across the room several times without stopping to keep warm. "Laugh at me my Sister [she wrote to Rebecca Seton, her sister-in-law], but it is very good exercise."[17] The smoke from the fire, when she could start it, aggravated William's blood-letting cough, as did the ever present drafts and dampness. Not surprisingly, Anna also began to develop a painful cough.

Then on November 30, a few dozen angry and hungry people of different nationalities arrived at the *lazaretto* after being shipwrecked. Elizabeth commented that some wore coats but no shirts, and others shirts but no coats. They were ushered into a nearby room that had, as Elizabeth described again with the faintest touch of humor, "naked walls, and the jug of water."[18] The noise of their fighting and quarrelling further tested the endurance of the Seton family. The man of authority in the *lazaretto*, the loyal *Capitano*, lacked the orders to solve the problem. He advised patience.[19]

Notwithstanding their hopeful expectations, the Setons encountered setback after setback on their journey, resulting in tragedy for the family. But even amid these rather dire circumstances, Anna noticed a difference that her mother had made possible, "For all we are so cold, and in this Prison Mamma, how happy we are compared with them [the people in the neighboring room] and we have peace, too."[20]

———•◆•———

In the *lazaretto*, Elizabeth's talents as an educator, leader, and caregiver began to take on heroic proportions. She adapted to the unforeseen circumstances and needs of her family. Her surroundings posed an additional level of insecurity. However, she provided a comforting and warm atmosphere in a painfully disagreeable and chilly room. Her gentle actions produced peace, compared to the chaos next door, and hope in the midst of despair.

The *lazaretto* room was an example of a domestic or house church. Her Christian family was a "community of faith, hope, and charity" (*CCC* no. 2204). Elizabeth, the enlightened and empowering educator, taught the faith by first setting a respectful atmosphere in which learning can take place. She used Scripture and prayer for her materials. The family shared love and fellowship.

Elizabeth, in the role of a liberating leader, demonstrated a hope for eternal life with God that was contagious. She took hope and, by trusting in God to lead the way, assured her family that her husband's suffering was not in vain. They looked forward to a better life without tears and sorrow.

As a charitable caregiver, Elizabeth showed her compassion and dedication in the many ways she nursed her dying husband. Some of those chores were extremely unpleasant, but she did not let frustrations or regrets prevent her from freely doing her best. (For example, she could have blamed herself or resented others for not considering the possibility of quarantine in Italy.) Her love for God and for her husband impelled her to put faith and hope into action. Only a woman blessed with the hidden virtues of humility, perseverance, self-control, and peace could transform such a wretched room into a place of domestic beauty where spiritual healing could take place. Those quiet virtues, practiced throughout her life, grew to become heroic virtues in the service of God.

——◆——

When the period of quarantine was over, the Setons were released from the *lazaretto* just before Christmas. The family immediately traveled to nearby Pisa to provide William with better health care. But the trip to Pisa and the comfort of new accommodations secured by the Filicchis came too late. William died within a week. Toward the end, he breathed out, "My dear Wife and little ones and My Christ Jesus have mercy and receive me...."[21] Then William's suffering was finally over. Elizabeth was exhausted. "His soul was released—and mine from a struggle next to death—"[22] In her anguish, she did not forget God.

I took my little Ann in my arms and made her kneel with me again by the dear Body, and thank our Heavenly Father for relieving him from his misery, for the Joyful assurance that through our Blessed Redeemer he had entered into Life Eternal, and implored his Protecting care and pity for us who have yet to finish our course.[23]

William was buried in the English burial ground in Livorno.* The Reverend Hall led the funeral service. The *Capitano* from the *lazaretto* attended. His gesture assuaged Elizabeth's raw emotions.[24] After the burial, Elizabeth and her daughter returned to Livorno to stay with the Filicchis. Her tired mind kept repeating, "My God, you are my God, and so I am now alone in the world with you and my little ones, but you are my Father and doubly theirs."[25]

The Filicchis were devoted Catholics, and during her five months in Italy, Elizabeth was drawn to their faith. To help relieve the Setons' grief, Amabilia Filicchi (Antonio's wife) took Elizabeth and Anna sightseeing. Elizabeth traveled to Florence and saw beautiful churches, art galleries, and museums. She also went to the opera, which she did not like.[26] During that time, Elizabeth learned about Saint Bernard's prayer to Mary, the Mother of Jesus, which is known as the *Memorare*. She was impressed by the prayer, and through it found the mother she had been searching for since childhood.[27] Filippo Filicchi enriched her spirituality by giving her a copy of

---

* Recently William Seton's grave has been moved to the church named after his wife in Livorno. Buried next to him, in the garden of the Parrocchia Madre Seton, is Antonio Filicchi—a sign of the value of enduring friendship.

Saint Francis de Sales' book, *Introduction to the Devout Life.* Later in life, Elizabeth would read the writings of Saint Francis' friend, Saint Louise de Marillac. Saint Louise became a role model, and Elizabeth was the first person to translate the saint's life from French into English.[28] The Filicchis also taught her to make the sign of the cross.

In February 1804, the Filicchis brought Elizabeth and Anna to a lovely place in the countryside of Tuscany: the sanctuary of the Benedictine Monastery in Montenero. The sanctuary sits at the top of a hill, Montenero, which means black mountain, about four miles from Livorno. The view from the hill top encompasses the city of Livorno and the aquamarine sea. At this elevation, the earth, sky and water seem limitless. The trip to Montenero would affect her remaining time in Italy.

The Filicchis visited Montenero to give thanks for the aid the monks had given Filippo Filicchi during a political revolution by hiding him in the monastery.[29] During her visit, Elizabeth attended a Mass. Her thoughts were interrupted by the words of an English-speaking visitor. When the host was elevated or raised during the prayers, he said, *"loud in my ear 'this is what they call their real PRESENCE.'"*[30] Elizabeth was deeply embarrassed that the young man could be so rude during this sacred moment in the silent church. The man's words made her uncomfortable and set off a chain reaction of confusing theological questions that challenged her Episcopal faith. God had grabbed her attention, and the words were in English (not Italian or Latin).

A portrait of the Blessed Virgin Mary, Our Lady of Montenero, the Patroness of Tuscany, hangs in the sanctuary. For centuries people had come to the sanctuary to ask Mary's intercession for their healing. Was Elizabeth's heart beginning to heal? We know that her soul was thrown into turmoil and overwhelmed.[31] That image of Mary, with the baby Jesus on her lap, may have prompted Elizabeth to think of her four younger children far across the ocean at home.

Elizabeth's visit to Montenero was one of many experiences that drew her to the Eucharist and the Catholic faith. It was a human, historic, and holy event. First, from the human point of view, Elizabeth reveals her reverence for the Eucharist. Despite his shortcomings the impolite young man very clearly pointed out to her the real presence in the Eucharist. The contrast of his loud words and the quiet adoration of the kneeling or prostrate congregation certainly burned this event into her memory. In her writing, Elizabeth used capital letters fairly sparingly. Therefore, one takes notice when she used them with the "*real* PRESENCE."

Second, from the historic point of view, her visit to Montenero was significant because it occurred before a setback in her life. Toward the end of February and the beginning of March, scarlet fever thwarted Elizabeth's plans to return to New York. Anna got sick, and then Elizabeth herself. They missed their boat. Another month passed before they could travel home. During this time, Elizabeth had more opportunities to experience Catholicism.

The compassion and care that the Filicchis continued to give her and her daughter prompted Elizabeth to reflect on their Christian charity.[32]

Finally, from the point of holiness, Montenero stirred Elizabeth's mind. Questions and confusion are natural on the road to conversion. For answers, Elizabeth looked to the example of the Filicchi family and their faith.

On April 8, 1804, Elizabeth and Anna sailed out of the port of Livorno on the *Pyomingo* for New York. Antonio Filicchi escorted them since he had business to attend to in the United States. As Elizabeth looked back at the west coast of Tuscany, she wrote, "Most dear Seton, where are you now? I lose sight of the shore that contains your dear ashes, and your soul is in that region of immensity where I cannot find you."[33]

• • • • • • • • • • •

CHAPTER FOUR

Conversion and Change

"Oh my God, forgive what I have been, correct what I am, and direct what I shall be."[1]

In June 1804 Elizabeth returned to her four younger children whom she had longed to see. They were well, and the family rejoiced that they were together again. The joyous reunion was dampened by the absence of William and the death of her sister-in-law, Rebecca, which occurred shortly after her arrival in New York. The thought looming over her was the unsettling question: "What now?"

The family's financial situation was worse than Elizabeth had thought.

> My Seton has left his five darlings and myself wholly dependent on the Bounty of those individuals who have loved and respected him. . . . Entirely unconscious of the desperate

state of his affairs, he died quite happy in the idea that we
would have a sufficiency when his books were brought up.
But on the contrary, there is even a great deficiency. . . .[2]

Her relatives were supporting her "for this year as my Rebecca
is so young, after which if I live I am to pursue some personal
exertion toward it myself—."[3]

It became clear that she would have to do something. One
solution would be to find a teaching position. Elizabeth had a
solid education and plenty of experience with her own children.
She had also helped to bring up William's younger siblings.
Another possibility for a woman such as Elizabeth would be to
marry again. Elizabeth's marriage to William was based on an
enduring love that had survived many trials. After William's
death, Elizabeth turned to God to fill the void in her heart. One
thing became certain for Elizabeth: she wished to be instructed
in the Catholic faith with the hope of converting.

Elizabeth's decision to convert was a gradual process. Subtle
spiritual gains were often counteracted with heart-wrenching
setbacks. She struggled to reconcile the Episcopal church of her
youth and marriage with her desire to join the Catholic Church.
In her words, "—the Scriptures once my delight and comfort are
now the continual sources of my pain, every page I open con-
founds my poor Soul, I fall on my knees and blinded with tears
cry out to God to teach me."[4] She did not wish to go against the
views of her spiritual director, the Reverend John Henry Hobart.
Elizabeth valued his friendship, but felt she had to do what was
right. She wrote in a draft of a letter, "if you[r] dear friendship
[Hobart] and esteem must be the price of my fidelity to what I
believe to be the truth—I cannot doubt the Mercy of God who

by depriving me of my dearest tie on earth will certainly draw me nearer to him. . . ."[5]

Her desire to convert also presented serious social and economic consequences. In 1804 Catholics usually belonged to the lower class, therefore aristocrats did not associate with them. Catholics were thought of as poor, uneducated, and unwashed. In converting to Catholicism, Elizabeth became increasingly isolated from the world she had always known. But by leaving her social and economic class, she was also free to pursue a new life. Still, it was a frightening experience that required great strength and the determination to endure much mental and physical suffering. With five young children to support, she acted at great risk. Elizabeth had to deal with her reduced financial circumstances in a city where several of her former friends and family members no longer welcomed her.

She had turned to teaching to support her family, but after her conversion, New York society feared she would convert their children. When her plans for a school failed, she was destitute.

The scorn of the people who had once loved and respected her came as a stinging blow to Elizabeth, who was a kind and cooperative woman. But she kept her faith and her head amid the bigotry and abuse. Some people from her past and family members remained life-long friends. A few of these loyal friends also helped her financially. But others tried to make her life miserable. When people looked down on her, however, she looked up to God. She understood that he would lead her in the right direction even if she was among strangers in the Catholic Church. "I seek but God and his church, and expect to find my peace in them, not in the people."[6]

Elizabeth Seton showed compassion and mercy to others, but she did not give in to the whims or demands of those who unjustly confronted her. It takes wisdom and self-control to do both. It is challenging to withstand criticism and continue to stand up for what you believe under stressful conditions. During this time, her children got sick and she had plenty of housework to do, making it difficult for her even to get to church. However, she knew that God was the ultimate, loving parent. He would not turn against her.

Obeying God meant submitting her will to his will. She aspired to accept this challenge. Her favorite prayer later in life was one of submission. She repeated it during the months before her death in 1821.[7] It was the prayer of Pope Pius VII: "May the most just, the most high and the most amiable will of God be in all things fulfilled, praised, and exalted above all forever."[8] But at this point in her spiritual journey, she needed assistance with submission and help to discern God's will. Elizabeth found guidance in the Catholic Church.

Elizabeth was increasingly drawn to the presence of the Eucharist in the Catholic Church. After she returned from Italy, she described how she was spiritually torn while attending the Episcopal Saint Paul's Church, not only a street but also a world away from Saint Peter's. She wrote to Amabilia Filicchi:

> I got in a side pew which turned my face towards the Catholic Church in the next street, and found myself twenty times speaking to the Blessed Sacrament there . . . tears plenty, and sighs as silent and deep as when I first entered your blessed Church of Annunciation in Florence, all turning to the one only desire to see the way most pleasing to my God, which ever that way is.[9]

After her conversion, she braved the icy winds and muddy streets of New York to walk to Saint Peter's Catholic Church. She remembered the scene with fondness: "ANNUNCIATION DAY: How bright the Sun these morning walks of preparation—deep snow, or smooth ice, all to me the same. I see nothing but the little bright cross on Saint Peter's Steeple."[10] Inside, Saint Peter's had a painting of the Crucifixion over the tabernacle.

All the suffering and sorrow she had experienced in life continued to reinforce her perseverance while her spiritual vision began to clear. She had been determined to learn about the Catholic faith for her own sake as well as her children's. Later in her life, she credits her stay in Italy with inspiring her to do this.

> I assure you my becoming a Catholic was a very simple consequence of going to a Catholic Country [Italy] where it was impossible for anyone interested in any religion, not to see the wide difference between the first established Faith given and founded by our Lord and his apostles, and the various forms it has since taken. . . .[11]

She had been drawn to the beauty of the Catholic Church in Italy. While she learned about the sacraments and teachings of the Church, she was also attracted to the interior beauty of the faith. Now Elizabeth was ready to act.

> It was the Knowledge of the Protestant Doctrine with regard to Faith, which made me a Catholic. . . . I was convinced my safe plan was to unite with the church in which, at all events, they admitted that I would find salvation, and where also I would be secure of the Apostolic Succession, as well as of the many consolations which no other religious but the Catholic can afford.[12]

When Elizabeth decided to become a Catholic, she did not regret it.

————•—•————

Elizabeth was received into the Catholic Church on March 14, 1805, and celebrated her first Holy Communion on March 25, 1805. She would later say that being able to receive the Eucharist often was "the greatest happiness on Earth."[13] Elizabeth understood the meaning of the Eucharist, and she fully experienced the joy as well. When she received her first Communion, she said, "GOD IS MINE and I AM HIS."[14] Her "first thought . . . was let God arise let his enemies be scattered,"[15] She knew her Psalms, and this is a quote from the first verse of Psalm 68. She went on, "Instead of the humble tender welcome I had expected to give him, it was a triumph of joy and gladness that the deliverer was come, and my defense and shield and strength and Salvation made mine for this World and the next—."[16]

The same Psalm portrays God as a "father of orphans and protector of widows . . ." (Ps 68:5). Elizabeth also cared about God's judgment. When she decided to become a Catholic, she wrote that she would be judged. She took responsibility for her children's faith as well as her own[17] and brought her children up as Catholics. She must have finally felt that she was truly in God's hands. He would take care of her and her children while on earth, and provide hope for eternity.

Now that she had converted, she felt "everything is easy. Poverty, suffering, displeasure of my friends all lead me to Him."[18] She also felt satisfied that her children would benefit from an upbringing lacking the excesses of wealth.[19] She wrote about simple joys such as playing the piano for her children while they danced. Such times helped her through the rougher days.

Elizabeth had also prayed to Mary for guidance to make the right decision for her young family.[20] And those prayers turned to joy. "Joy to be Catholics—Zeal for the honor of Mary— Pleasing Jesus much by pleasing her in faithful service of love, prayer and homage to her and especially by continual remembrance and imitation of her Virtues."[21]

Conversion also coincided with the reconciliation of some family members. Elizabeth attended her stepmother, Charlotte Bayley, when she died in the summer of 1805. It gave Elizabeth great joy to heal with service the past wounds of human alienation.[22]

—•—

Elizabeth found friendship in the saints, with her close friends, and with William Magee Seton's stepsisters, the confidants and soul sisters who would die in Emmitsburg. In her Spiritual Journal to her sister-in-law, Cecilia Seton, Elizabeth once wrote on the feast of Saint Teresa of Ávila:

> Holy Mother you called yourself a Sinner—the worst of Sinners—What then am I—the sins of your whole Life would be balanced by the sum of any one of my days— . . . Blessed saints of God pray for the wandering weary soul who has stayed so far behind. You have reached the Summit— pray for me.[23]

Here a future saint, bogged down by the memory of her imperfections, prays for the intercession of heavenly saints while writing to her earthly friend.

Elizabeth valued friendship and shared her faith and soul in her letters. She had common sense and a fine-tuned sense of perspective. Her selflessness provided the light and air for friendships to grow.

At times in her life Elizabeth also needed the comfort of friendship. In 1806, she wrote to her friend, Julia Scott. "My dear friend you surely know that your steady unremitting affection in my worldly shipwreck is a sweet consolation, and one of the very few remaining endearments of this life."[24] She also understood the value of long lasting friendship. "I find in proportion as my heart is more drawn towards the summit, it looks backward with added tenderness to everyone I have ever loved, much more those who have long possessed its entire and truest attachment."[25]

Elizabeth's legacy is a legacy of love. Her love for God always came first, and her love of her neighbor followed. She recognized God in others, and she responded by loving them and helping them. By means of her sanctity and intercession in heaven, her friendship to all on earth knows no boundaries. She lived the words of Jesus so that others may know the hope of eternal life. "You shall love the Lord your God with all your heart, and with all your soul, and with all your strength, and with all your mind; and your neighbor as yourself" (Lk 10:27).

In May 1806, Elizabeth received the sacrament of Confirmation from Bishop John Carroll of Baltimore during his visit to Saint Peter's Church. He noticed her valiant struggle, determination, and commitment to persevere. A member of an influential and wealthy Maryland family, he could identify with this woman who continued to sacrifice the search for worldly wealth in exchange for spiritual wealth. He deeply respected her.

In 1807, the Reverend Louis William Valentine Dubourg, the President of Saint Mary's College in Baltimore, also visited New York and met Elizabeth. After discussing her plans for the future, he invited Elizabeth to come to Baltimore to start a Catholic school for girls. Bishop John Carroll approved the invitation, and Reverend Dubourg made the arrangements. These plans included keeping her two sons, William and Richard, at Georgetown College, which at that time took boys as boarders. Bishop Carroll had helped with making the arrangements for their admission in 1806 and for securing their tuition.[26] In the end, Antonio Filicchi offered to pay their tuition.[27]

Elizabeth had little to gain by staying in New York. Her urgent need to support her young Catholic family was also a factor in her decision to go to Baltimore. Her mind was made up. In a letter to Antonio Filicchi, Elizabeth noted Father Dubourg's words, "Come to us, Mrs. Seton, we will assist you in forming a plan of life."[28] To which she said, "I objected only [for] want of talents to which he replied we want example more than talents."[29] And so, in June 1808, Elizabeth followed God's call to Maryland.

CHAPTER FIVE

Baltimore: Answering God's Call

"I am in your hands my God—."[1]

On March 24, 1634, the day before the Feast of the Annunciation of the Blessed Virgin Mary, passengers from two English ships, the *Ark* and the *Dove*, reached the shores of the Colony of Maryland. The newly arrived Jesuit priest, Father Andrew White, celebrated the first Catholic Mass in Maryland on March 25. Thus Maryland began as being tolerant to the Catholic faith. Although Maryland Day marks the arrival of the *Ark* and the *Dove* each year on March 25, Catholics also remember the Blessed Virgin Mary on this day.

Over 150 years later, in 1789, a series of events occurred in Baltimore, New York, Washington, D.C., and Europe, which related personally to Elizabeth and William Seton. During their marriage, the Setons circulated in the social crowd of

newly-elected President George Washington. John Carroll
became the Bishop of Baltimore, the first Catholic diocese in the
United States. This diocese originally included all thirteen colonies and later grew to encompass the area of the Louisiana
Purchase. Meanwhile, across the Atlantic in Italy, the Filicchis
established their mercantile business, which helped to secure the
Baltimore Diocese.

> Early in 1789 as a result of the meeting between Philip
> [Filippo] Filicchi and John Carroll, Antonio Filicchi and
> William Magee Seton, who was then visiting in Italy, called
> on Rev. John Thorpe, Carroll's friend in Rome. During their
> discussion about the difficulty of satisfactory communica-
> tion between Baltimore and Rome, Seton suggested using
> the trade route established between his father's firm and the
> Filicchis' as a mail channel. The letter containing Rome's
> permission for the American clergy to select their own see
> city and to nominate their choice for the first bishop of the
> United States reached Carroll, via the Filicchis in Leghorn
> [Livorno] and the Setons in New York.[2]

It was providential that the Filicchis knew Bishop Carroll
and continued to correspond with him about Elizabeth after the
death of her husband, during her conversion in New York, and
beyond. Without William Magee Seton, this may have been
impossible.

The beginning of the French Revolution in 1789 drove some
priests of the Society of Saint Sulpice (founded in Paris in 1641)
to Baltimore. These newly arrived Sulpicians joined the staff of
Saint Mary's Seminary, the first Catholic Seminary in the United
States, which was established in Baltimore's French quarter in
1791. In 1808 Elizabeth Seton arrived in Baltimore to start her

first Catholic school for girls on the grounds of Saint Mary's. In nearby Washington, in 1789, John Carroll established Georgetown College, attended by Elizabeth's two sons from 1806 to 1808.

And what was Elizabeth doing in 1789? She was on the shores of Long Island Sound undergoing a profound spiritual experience that brought her to the realization that God was her Father. On that spring day, when God forged a new bond with her soul, he was also weaving the circumstances of Elizabeth's destiny. Domestic and foreign events during the year 1789 intersected and converged with her story.

It is an extraordinary fact that William Magee Seton worked with John Carroll before he even knew Elizabeth. And when John Carroll met Elizabeth in 1806, she might have known that her husband had helped to safeguard the letter that created the Catholic diocese.

Having met William Seton, Bishop Carroll would have been fully aware of Elizabeth's background. Her fine education, manners, deportment and social skills enabled her to gently counteract the unfair, anti-Catholic sentiments of the time. Bishop Carroll had found the woman to lead the first community of American Catholic Sisters.

Elizabeth was also well connected to every class of people. She had learned in Italy that rich and poor could freely worship together in a Catholic church. As a convert, she had done the same. That experience of no prejudice would help her establish a spirit of equality and freedom in her Catholic schools and American Sisters of Charity. She also had the perfect resumé for her vocation. Her experience as treasurer of the Society for the

Relief of Poor Widows with Small Children in New York gave her a background in administration and the financial skills of stewardship and fund raising.[3] All of Elizabeth's experience would serve her well as she embarked on her new mission in Baltimore.

———•◆•———

In 1808 Baltimore was the third largest city in America, and its port was vital to the United States. When the British attacked the harbor six years later during the War of 1812, it was because they understood it provided a gateway to the north, to the south, and to Europe. Baltimore is south of the Mason Dixon line, but it retains climatic and other characteristics of both north and south. Unlike New York City, the port of Baltimore has never been occupied by a foreign power.

Elizabeth and her three daughters arrived in Baltimore's Inner Harbor in June of 1808. The trip from New York City to Baltimore aboard the *Grand Sachem* took approximately a week. The fare for the mother and three daughters was $50.00.[4] The rough voyage inspired many prayers until they entered the Chesapeake Bay, when "a fairer wind and lighter hearts"[5] changed the mood of the trip. The girls sang and snacked on almonds and raisins, and everyone was treated to a glorious sunset over the bay.

After a night on board the ship in the Fells Point area of Baltimore's harbor, Elizabeth and her daughters traveled about two miles by carriage the next day to Saint Mary's Seminary. Naturally excited and perhaps nervous about her new home,

Elizabeth wrote to her sister-in-law, Cecilia Seton, "... doubt and fear fly from the heart inhabited by him—there can be no disappointment where the Souls only desire and expectation is to meet his Adored Will and fulfill it."[6] Because of her faith in God, she hoped and trusted that all would be well, as Scripture teaches us: "Now faith is the assurance of things hoped for, the conviction of things not seen" (Heb 11:1). And "hope does not disappoint us, because God's love has been poured into our hearts through the Holy Spirit that has been given to us" (Rom 5:5).

The Setons arrived at the Chapel of Saint Mary's Seminary on the Feast of Corpus Christi (the Body of Christ) on June 16, 1808. The Eucharist had drawn Elizabeth to the Catholic faith, and her arrival to her new home and school on Corpus Christi would have been enough of a reason to celebrate. But there was more. The dedication Mass for the new Chapel was in progress when she arrived, and she was thrilled to immediately participate in the celebration. Bishop Carroll presided over the Mass and greeted the family afterward. Scarred by the religious persecution she had experienced in New York, she was deeply moved to be welcomed by Baltimore's Catholic community. She describes the scene: "surrounded by so many caresses and Blessings—all my wonder is how I got through it—the Darlings [her daughters] confounded with wonder and delight ..."[7]

—•—

A few days after Elizabeth arrived at Saint Mary's and before her school opened, she traveled to Georgetown College in Washington to bring her two sons back to Baltimore. She traveled with Father Michael Hurley and Samuel Cooper, a wealthy, retired sea captain and future priest. Elizabeth and her daughters had not seen William and Richard in two years. When the Seton boys arrived at Saint Mary's, they were enrolled in the college on the grounds of the Sulpician seminary. Elizabeth, a wise mother with a sense of humor, predicted that the happy mood of her children's reunion would not last too long. "The children are in a dream of delight on being once more united . . . but . . . it is all a novelty and consequently bears its best appearance [and] it is liable to change."[8]

The Setons' new house on Paca Street was a "delightful mansion . . . entirely new, in the French style of folding windows and recesses . . ."[9] "placed between two orchards, and two miles from the city."[10] The two-and-a-half story federal-style house was probably designed by Maximilian Godefroy (who designed the Chapel). It was a small, elegant house with a fireplace in each comfortable room. The first floor had a kitchen, a sitting area, and a formal parlor. The second floor probably contained a craft room and two other rooms with alcoves for Elizabeth's bedroom and the schoolroom. The simple third floor accommodated the girls (Elizabeth's three daughters and seven student boarders) in the federal-style rope beds of the times. A smaller room at the back of the third floor could have been used for storage. Elizabeth loved her "dear little dwelling."[11] Even the winding, delicate, low-rising staircase with "lady treads" and an apple-wood banister were perfectly suited to the all-female household and the four-foot eleven-inch Elizabeth. But above all she valued its location near the chapel and loved living in a community of spirituality and "Divine Charity."[12] In a letter to Antonio Filicchi, she wrote of the "chapel the most elegant in America . . . so near my dwelling that I can hear the bell at the altar—Oh Filicchi: you, who knew so well how [to] pity your Sister will gladly receive the account of this happy reverse."[13]

Setting up her school involved a great deal of work. As a mother living in her workplace around the clock, she had to get organized quickly. She still found time to write to her friend Julia Scott that "it indeed has been next to impossible to write—after our arrival here I went immediately to Washington for my dear Boys, and having my family to settle, house to arrange, clothes to repair and such heat. . . ."[14] Even in 1808, with the breezes blowing through the apple orchards around her house, Elizabeth was like anyone who had moved from a cooler climate to Baltimore. The hot, humid summers are quite a shock to the system. Fortunately, the cost of living was lower in Baltimore than in New York. Her rent in New York had been 350 dollars for a larger home and 150 dollars for a place that had "five in a room and closet."[15] She rented her substantial house in Baltimore for only 200 dollars.[16] She also saved money on food, furniture, clothes for her children, and wood for cooking and heat. The seminary bought things in bulk, which made a "difference of at least a third less expense in every Article."[17] She engaged a lay woman to help with the usual laundry, cooking, and cleaning, which kept the domestic chaos under control. Finally the school was ready.

A Catholic education remained the focus of Elizabeth's new school. The girls attended chapel in the early morning and in the evening, when they took time for an examination of conscience and prayed the rosary.[18] The students were taught reading, grammar, and arithmetic, as well as music and drawing by the seminary teachers. They learned the skills of sewing and needlepoint. In their spare time, they visited the homes of acquaintances and walked around town.

In October 1808 Elizabeth wrote that ". . . it is expected that I shall be the Mother of many daughters."[19] The "daughters" referred to the community of Catholic sisters that was beginning to take root under Elizabeth's leadership. This group would become the Sisters of Charity of Saint Joseph's in Emmitsburg. The main model for the American Sisters of Charity was the French Daughters of Charity. Founded in France in 1633 by Saint Vincent de Paul and Saint Louise de Marillac (another wealthy widow and mother), the French Daughters of Charity exemplified the mission of charity and service to the poor. Saint Vincent de Paul believed that these religious sisters should work among the poor and sick, educate in schools, and worship in parish churches.[20]

In 1850, the community of the Sisters of Charity in Emmitsburg united with the Daughters of Charity in Paris, and the Emmitsburg community became the Daughters of Charity. Both the American Sisters and Daughters of Charity have established communities in the United States and abroad, but they all trace their origins back to Mother Seton's original community in Emmitsburg. Today these communities retain the charitable spirit of Saint Vincent de Paul and continue to serve others in the Setonian tradition.

The Catholic Church in Baltimore offered Elizabeth an opportunity to be a pioneer in the fields of Catholic education and social services, and she rose to the occasion. She would face struggles, but she felt "afflictions are the steps to heaven."[21] As for the successes, she gave all credit to God. Her work was for his greater glory. She wished to "mount to thee by the stairs of Humility on which thou camest down to me."[22] She always remembered that Jesus "was born for me in a stable, lived for me a life of pain and sorrow, and died for me upon a cross."[23]

Historically, Elizabeth was in the right place at the right time. She was developing new connections and friends who shared her Catholic faith. Freed from the prejudices and restrictions that can accompany social standing and wealth, Elizabeth gathered women based on their desire to join a mission of faith and service. From the human perspective, Baltimore had given her a new lease on life. The Sulpician community offered her the chance to rest from the rejection and antagonism she had faced in New York. She now had a promising job that gave her some financial stability. She was no longer totally dependent upon her friends for her family's livelihood. As for the spiritual part of her life, Elizabeth found much nourishment for her soul living in the Sulpician community. She also had the support of the leadership of the Catholic Church in the United States and was part of its vision. In Baltimore, she wrote to a friend that she was ". . . breathing the air of Peace and tranquility in the atmosphere she loves."[24] Her vocation, focused on God, was solidified as well. In her words, "the thirst and longing of my soul is fixed on the cross alone."[25]

On March 25, 1809, the Feast of the Annunciation of the Blessed Virgin Mary, Elizabeth Seton privately pronounced her temporary vows of chastity and obedience as a Catholic sister in front of Bishop John Carroll in the Lower Chapel of Saint Mary's Seminary.* He was the first to call her Mother Seton. In June 1809, the four candidates of her small community appeared in their habits, which were an adopted form of Mother Seton's Italian widow's costume. They wore black dresses and capes, and white caps trimmed with a black band to secure them.[26] The sisters set a promising example of virtue, which provided solid hope for the future.

Appropriately, Elizabeth would become Mother Seton and pronounce her first vows in the Chapel of the Presentation of the Blessed Virgin Mary in the Temple. In presenting the child Mary in the temple, her parents were offering hope to all people. Like Mary, Elizabeth humbly and courageously accepted God's will. Also like Mary, she is remembered as a mother.

In June of 1809, Elizabeth's sisters-in-law, Cecilia and Harriet Seton, traveled from New York to join her at Saint Mary's. Their reunion would be tragically short, since both Cecilia and Harriet died within a year.

Baltimore closed one chapter in Elizabeth's life and began another. Although each phase of her life includes human, historic, and holy stories, dimensions within those stories are more

---

* Today, St. Mary's Spiritual Center and Historic Site, www.stmarys spiritual center.org, is home to the original seminary chapel (known as the Presentation of the Blessed Virgin Mary in the Temple) and the Mother Seton House.

pronounced in certain places. In New York, the human dimensions stand out when her life changed from wife and mother to widow and convert. In Baltimore, the historic aspects of widow and convert converge to solidify her new vocation. And it would be in Emmitsburg that her vocation would grow and become glorified.

. . . .

CHAPTER SIX

From Emmitsburg to Eternity

"Our God loves US that is our comfort."[1]

But first, Elizabeth needs to move on to Emmitsburg. Samuel Cooper, the retired sea captain who helped escort her to Georgetown in June 1808, assisted her again on a new journey. He purchased 269 acres of farmland about fifty miles northwest of Baltimore for her community.[2] The decision to relocate to Emmitsburg became clear. It can be summed up in one word: proceed.

In June 1809, Mother Seton, as she was now known, and a small group of religious sisters left Baltimore for the pastoral setting of Emmitsburg, Maryland. The women mostly walked along the side of a Conestoga wagon, which carried supplies, furniture, and the ailing Cecilia Seton.[3] Major roads did not go all the way to Emmitsburg at that time, and some of the way was rough and primitive.

Toward the end of the approximately fifty-mile journey, the Catoctin Mountains emerged in the horizon in gently rolling blue waves. The hills closer to the travelers slowly turned green when the trees came into focus. Wild flowers, such as Queen Anne's lace, dotted the fields and woodland. The wind blew like the boundless wind at sea. It tossed about the various shades of long, green grass under an expansive sky. In the surrounding beauty, it was easy to lift up the heart to God. But the determined group also gained ground despite the hardships of the trip. Because it was Maryland in June, the breezes must have brought relief from the hot sun and humidity.

This was perhaps the third time in her life that Elizabeth faced mountainous terrain. On each of these occasions she also faced momentous changes in her life. The first time, after she passed Gibraltar, she became a widow. The second time, descending from the hill at Montenero, her soul was filled with thoughts and feelings about the Blessed Sacrament, which would eventually inspire her to convert to Catholicism. Finally, next to the mountains in Emmitsburg, Maryland, her vocation as an educator and foundress took root and grew to be glorified. With each unknown, she surpassed expectations and human predictions. When she approached Emmitsburg, she looked to the future. As always, God was her companion who led the way in the present.

Elizabeth's playful nature comes through in an account of the trip; ". . . the dogs and pigs came out to meet us and the geese stretched their necks in mute demand to know if we were any of their sort to which we gave assent."[4]

Arriving at the College and Seminary of Mount Saint Mary's, Elizabeth was greeted by the Sulpician priest Reverend John Dubois. He had founded the college and became its president in 1808. Because the house was not ready, the women stayed in a log cabin on the college property. The primitive cabin was on the side of the mountain overlooking the valley. This view might have reminded Elizabeth of the spectacular panorama from Montenero in Italy. Although Emmitsburg is not on the seacoast, looking out over the valley brings peace to the soul. Elizabeth delighted in the location of her temporary home, commenting: ". . . we were half in the sky the height of our situation is almost incredible."[5]

Elizabeth, her religious sisters, and her own five children had all arrived in Emmitsburg by the end of July. Her sons, William and Richard, were enrolled in the College of Mount Saint Mary's, located at the foot of the mountain not far from her new home in Saint Joseph's Valley.

On July 31, 1809, the feast day of Saint Ignatius of Loyola, Elizabeth founded the first order of American Catholic Sisters, known as the Sisters of Charity of Saint Joseph's, in Emmitsburg.

Around this date, the women and children (sixteen in all) moved into a two story, four-room farmhouse known as the Stone House.[6] Beds were in short supply, and as the weather turned colder, snow often drifted down through the cracks in the house onto the women who slept on the floor. The inadequate food and overcrowding inevitably resulted in sickness and death. Elizabeth's sister-in-law, Harriet, died just before Christmas.

Despite the hardships, the little community of sisters taught lessons to the children, established and followed strict daily schedules of manual labor and chores, and set aside specific times for worship and prayer. Elizabeth felt order was important and activity was healthy, ". . . [E]xperience has convinced me I must always be doing something and the more I exert the better for mind and body."[7] "Doing something" included spiritual activities as well. It was also a practical way to alleviate worry and thoughts of despair. But she could not do it all. Even as the leader of a community, Elizabeth humbly realized when it was better to give a task to someone more capable of carrying it out. "If you are to do his work, the strength will be given you; if not . . . someone else will do it."[8]

In 1810, the women moved into the new, larger White House before the construction was completed. The first high Mass was offered in the chapel on the Feast of Saint Joseph (March 19).[9] Also, in 1810, Mother Seton established Saint Joseph's Free School in the White House. It was the first free Catholic girls' school run by religious sisters in the United States. As the school grew, some students paid tuition for another new school, Saint Joseph's Academy, which was established later in 1810. It was staffed by her religious sisters and included boarders.[10] The tuition from the students at Saint Joseph's Academy helped to fund the free school.

In January 1812 (on the Feast Day of Saint Sulpice), the community adopted rules based on those of the Daughters of Charity of Saint Vincent de Paul in France. Elizabeth and her religious sisters made their first vows in July 1813.[11] The community's mission suited the needs of the growing Catholic Church in America. Its purpose was to seek out the physically and spiritually poor and to serve them, particularly through education.

Mother Seton was a pioneer in American Catholic education. In those days, young women were home schooled, had tutors, or were enrolled in private Catholic or non-Catholic schools. The free school Elizabeth started in Emmitsburg differed from other Catholic schools in the early 1800s. While the girls at her Catholic school in Baltimore had to pay tuition, Mother Seton dreamed of making a difference by offering a Catholic education to anyone regardless of what people could pay for it. Since it was necessary for Elizabeth to charge tuition for the students at Saint Joseph's Academy, her dream was only partially fulfilled in Emmitsburg.

Her small community of sisters expanded to Philadelphia in 1814. Later they would expand throughout the United States and around the world. Three of her sisters set out for New York City in 1817, where they opened a Roman Catholic orphanage. In the next 200 years, her Sisters and Daughters of Charity branched out to found more orphanages, child care organizations, hospitals, and social welfare organizations in the Untied States and around the globe. Today her legacy has spread worldwide, fulfilling her words, "I am a citizen of the world."[12]

———•———

Elizabeth's five children spent most of their teenage years in Emmitsburg. Parents and teachers of teenagers know emerging adults need plenty of care. You have to recognize when to offer advice or let things take their course. Gentle discipline requires wisdom and patience as children acquire independence. Being a good role model for an adolescent takes time. Elizabeth was a loving and responsible mother who put her children's welfare first. She was also a single mother who needed to make her position and priorities clear to her superiors.

> . . . [T]he dear ones have their first claim which must ever remain inviolate. Consequently, if at any period, the duties I am engaged in should interfere with those I owe to them, I have solemnly engaged with our good Bishop John Carroll, as well as my own conscience, to give the darlings their right, and to prefer their advantage in everything.[13]

This was not the typical situation for a superior of religious sisters. Elizabeth's strong language emphasized that she meant what she said. She had the foresight to protect her children and the capability to carry out her intentions. It could not have been easy to decipher her children's daily needs while living day and night with other people's children and in a community of sisters. She did the best should could. And sometimes the best was tiring. "Faith lifts the staggering soul on one side, Hope supports it on the other, experience says it must be—and love says let it be."[14]

The hardest challenges Elizabeth faced in Emmitsburg involved her children. About the time the *Rules and Constitutions of the Sisters of Charity in the United States* were confirmed in the early days of 1812, Elizabeth's Anna became desperately ill. Elizabeth was consoled when her devout and saintly daughter Anna was happily consecrated as a Sister of Charity of Saint Joseph's on her deathbed. However, when Anna died of tuberculosis at the age of sixteen, Elizabeth was shattered. ". . . For three months after Nina [Anna or Annina] was taken, I was so often expecting to lose my senses and my head was so disordered that unless for the daily duties always before me I did not know much of what I did or what I left undone."[15] Like other parents before and after her, Elizabeth healed slowly while she struggled to accept the present and a future without her oldest child.

Elizabeth could not have foreseen how Anna's illness and her preoccupation with nursing a dying child would have even more tragic consequences. During the winter of 1812, Elizabeth's youngest child, Rebecca, fell on the ice. Reluctant to worry her preoccupied mother about the painful fall, Rebecca suffered in silence. Soon the pain became obvious, and by that time the injury proved critical. Rebecca's condition deteriorated over the next four years.

Toward the end, Elizabeth held her daughter day and night for nine weeks, "even eating my meal with one hand often behind her pillow while she rested on my knees—her pains could find no relief or solace but in her own poor Mother so happy to bear them with her. . . ."[16] Elizabeth developed a form of tendonitis from this exertion. The painful condition lasted for months after Rebecca's death, at the age of fourteen, in November 1816.[17] Rebecca was buried next to her sister Anna in the graveyard in view of the White House. In a letter to her son William, Elizabeth wrote of Rebecca's last days: ". . . it is not possible to give you a true idea of the Virtues of Rebecca, her beauty of Soul and body increased daily even to the arms of Death."[18]

Elizabeth recovered more quickly from her youngest child's death. During the illness and death of both children, she received consolation and guidance from her spiritual director, Reverend Simon Gabriel Bruté. He was a Sulpician priest, born in France in 1779. He met Elizabeth in 1811, and with her fluent command of French, she helped him to improve his English. Their friendship grew, and they nurtured each other's souls. Reverend Bruté advised her during the rest of her life and was with her the day she died.[19]

The friendship between Mother Seton and Simon Bruté continues into this century. In the summer of 2004, I had the privilege of meeting members of the Bruté family and attending Mass with them, when they came from France and visited the Mother Seton House and Old Saint Mary's Seminary Chapel in Baltimore. Reverend Bruté was the president of Saint Mary's College on Paca Street from around 1815 to 1818.

Life goes on, and the Emmitsburg school continued to thrive. In addition to the Catholic faith, the sisters taught classes that included reading, writing, grammar, spelling, geography, arithmetic, music, and French. Elizabeth did not discriminate between rich and poor children. She respected and gently corrected her students while keeping the standards high for all. Sometimes parents disagreed with her, but she knew how to handle them.

Elizabeth's sons, however, provided fresh dilemmas. The "saucy boys [who] almost master me,"[20] grew into young men who naturally wished to make their own way in the world. The Filicchis offered to have both William and Richard stay in Italy, where they would learn about their shipping business. The boys also benefited from their example. In return, Elizabeth and her religious sisters prayed for the Filicchis.[21]

In a letter to her son William, who was in Italy, Elizabeth expressed her concern that he remember to respect the people (the Filicchis) who provided their financial support. "You will mind economy in Everything, as we have Nothing but what we receive from our friends, till you make your own independence

my William."[22] She also wrote to "not give way to National prejudices, but to allow for many customs and manners you will see."[23]
She was most concerned about his soul, and reminded him to do
the will of God and to be charitable to others. But also being a
sensible mother, she warns him not to be "duped" by strangers,
while cautioning him never to make fun of them. She closes her
letter by reminding William again to watch his finances by keeping a list of expenditures. Finally, joining the plea of mothers
throughout time, she asks him to "give her the fullest account of
all that happens to you" and not "to omit your prayers on any
account."[24]

Of course the boys had a few plans of their own, which
apparently did not include writing home on a regular basis.
Money was spent quickly, and Elizabeth worried about their
behavior and their futures. Both boys eventually joined the
United States Navy. Richard served as a captain's clerk on the
U.S.S. Cyane after his mother's death. He selflessly and success-
fully attended a shipmate, the U.S. Consul Jehudi Ashmun
during his illness. But Richard's actions proved fatal. He caught
the same fever and died. He was buried at sea near the coast of
Liberia in June of 1823.[25]

William served in the U.S. Navy from 1818 to 1834 as a
midshipman and later as a lieutenant.[26] His mother kept a record
of his travels by chartering them on a globe. She continued to
pour out her love for him in her letters. William was the only
child who married and had children. He is buried at Mount Saint
Mary's in Emmitsburg.

There are no direct descendants of Elizabeth and William
Seton alive today. However, Elizabeth's step-nephew, James

Roosevelt Bayley, followed his aunt's example of service to the church and became the eighth Catholic Archbishop of Baltimore. His magnificent cross is now at the Cathedral of Mary Our Queen in Baltimore. It is carried down the long aisle on special celebrations such as Christmas and Easter. A grandson, Robert Seton, also became an archbishop.

Her middle child, Catherine, joined the Sisters of Mercy and worked with prisoners.

She was the only child present at her mother's death. Catherine died in New York City at the age of 90.

———•◆•———

The Eucharist sustained and fortified Elizabeth after her conversion and increased her ability to cope with the many trials she faced in Emmitsburg. It was her spiritual anchor and sextant both in the calm and in the deep, stormy seas of life. "I sit or stand opposite his tabernacle all day, and keep the heart to it as the needle to the pole."[27] The physical presence of the Eucharist within her added another dimension to Elizabeth's personal relationship with Christ. "A true joy to me indeed the daily morning Sacrifice [Mass] and our frequent and daily communion, when prepared—what a contrast to the morning sleep in former days. It has been my Wealth in Poverty, and joy in deepest afflictions."[28]

By increasing her awareness of the presence of Christ within her life, she acquired an even greater ability to recognize Christ in others. As God increased in her, she decreased, so as to allow more space for him. This is what John the Baptist meant by saying of

Jesus, "He must increase, but I must decrease" (Jn 3:30). The spirit of God was revealed to others by the love of God in her heart.

If the Eucharist was her spiritual compass, God's will supplied direction and purpose. But first she had to submit her will to God's will. Submission was difficult, but the results produced much value in her life. It gave her the freedom to be the person God created her to be. In this perfected form of freedom, she used her gifts and talents to serve others instead of indulging herself or her pride. Her words proved that she tried to follow the path that God had planned for her. "The first end I propose in our daily work is to do the will of God—secondly, to do it in the manner he wills it—and thirdly, to do it because it is his will."[29]

Elizabeth understood discipleship and its cost. One source of frustration came from an unlikely source. Her patience was tried when her second superior in Emmitsburg,[30] the Reverend John Baptist David, made life difficult for her. He gave orders without fully consulting Elizabeth, and she did not agree with him.[31] Elizabeth realized that working in the Church is not a solitary, spiritual experience, and that she was participating in the larger mission of the Church. She also wisely understood that the Church is made up of imperfect people. In retrospect, we can see that both Reverend David and Elizabeth tried to do what they thought was right in the eyes of God.

Eventually the Reverend David moved to Kentucky, and his exit solved the problem for Elizabeth.[32] Years earlier, Reverend David had comforted Elizabeth when her sister-in-law, Harriet Seton, died in 1809. His words could have been applied to their future conflict, although neither he nor Elizabeth would have anticipated this.

> Let us adore the unsearchable, but always wise and merciful
> ways of Providence; and let us more than ever convince our-
> selves, that Jesus wishes to be the sole possessor of our hearts,
> to abandon themselves with perfect resignation into his
> Hands . . . having no other thought, in troublesome and
> painful encounters, than to submit lovingly to whatever
> God will be pleased to ordain.[33]

As Elizabeth approached middle age, her health weakened. Never robust, the stress and ailments of the past caught up with her. In the fall of 1820, she started to decline. Always thinking of others, she now had to humbly accept the charity and care of her religious sisters.[34] She wrote: "The virtues of the infirm are meekness, humility, patience, resignation, and gratitude for help received."[35] As the new year of 1821 dawned, Elizabeth's physical strength ebbed rapidly.

Toward the end of her life, Elizabeth wrote, "With what a lively, cheerful heart we go to work, even when the thing we are to do displeases poor nature, if only grace cries out courageously, 'it is all for you, my God.'"[36] She had almost completed her mission on earth, doing everything for the One who was everything to her. On January 4, 1821, she died in her bedroom at Emmitsburg and was welcomed into the arms of her Eternal Father. Originally buried near her daughters, Elizabeth's relics are now in the basicila at her national shrine in Emmitsburg.

In 1907, James Cardinal Gibbons began Mother Seton's cause for sainthood. Three required miracles were authenticated over the next six decades. The first miracle was for Sister Gertrude Korzendorfer of New Orleans, who was cured of pancreatic cancer. Ann O'Neill, a Catholic child from Baltimore, was the second miracle. She was healed of leukemia through the intercession of Mother Seton. The final miracle was for Carl Eric Kalin, a Protestant from New York, who was healed of a fatal brain disease. The miracles were worked for people who exemplified aspects of Mother Seton's life—a religious sister, a Catholic child from Baltimore, and a Protestant from New York.

On September 14, 1975, Pope Paul VI canonized Elizabeth Ann Bayley Seton, the first native-born United States Roman Catholic saint. Her feast day is January 4, the day her eternal life began.

————•◆•————

Two days before she died, Elizabeth had told her religious sisters to "be children of the Church."[37] The Catholic Church gave Elizabeth the opportunity to create, build, and lead a community of sisters, and the support to make it thrive. She laid the foundation for a Catholic school managed by religious sisters, which would help to establish the network of parochial schools in the United States. She was able to use all her gifts of wisdom, administration, and pastoral care in the service of the Church, at a time when women were not typically entrepreneurs and leaders in the secular world. Through the Church, a woman of faith such as Elizabeth could see her dreams come true. The universality of the Church would also provide what was necessary for the future mission of her sisters.

Elizabeth was devoted to Mary, the Queen of All Saints, who possesses the virtues of all the saints. Each saint has his or her gifts and talents and lived an exemplary life of faith. But Mary exceeds them all. Conceived without sin, Mary represents the perfect example of humility and obedience to God. Thus, by telling her sisters to be children of the Church, Elizabeth put them under the protection of Mary as well.

Elizabeth upheld the teachings of the Catholic Church and believed these would lead to eternal life. She also believed that the Eucharist connected all people throughout the earth by the real presence of the body and blood of Jesus. She valued that connection, which erased the man-made barriers of race, class, politics, and wealth. The fruit of her work brought joy, hope, healing, and promise. When she cried out for God's help during her conversion, God responded by helping not only her but also others through her.[38] Her dream continues today in the charitable work of her sisters. Catholic schools offer an option for educating children in the faith. As a canonized saint, she offers the gift of her intercession for anyone who asks for it.

As a mother the Church nurtures all people in the faith; for in the Church, all are one. In a similar way, the universality of Elizabeth's legacy is represented in churches across the globe.[39] For example, the statue of Saint Elizabeth Ann Seton in Saint Patrick's Cathedral in New York City (removed during the Cathedral's current restoration) was a copy of the statue at the entrance of the Parrocchia Madre Seton in Livorno.

Elizabeth's humanity, history, and holiness are timeless. The Catholic Church has preserved her memory for the edification of others. The first native saint from the United States, who called God her Father, knew how to leave all she valued on earth in his hands.

This valiant woman had no roadmap to guide her. She endured the humiliation of bankruptcy as a wife and the resulting financial insecurity as a widow. Because of her conversion to Catholicism, she was forced into a form of self-inflicted social quarantine from the people who once accepted her. Without losing ground, she remained focused and productive. She stood up for what she knew was right for her life, even though it did not look right to society. Elizabeth had lost her money, buried her husband in a distant land, and withstood the scorn of family and friends because of a deeply revealing and personal decision to convert to Catholicism. She faced poverty and the terrifying prospect of bringing up her five young children in uncertainty. As she gradually shed the material and comfortable attachments of her former life, she gained a detachment of soul. It became even more necessary to trust in God and to accept the present with an open and willing heart. In her words, ". . . all gone forever . . . My Husband, my sisters, my Home, my comforts— Poverty and sorrow—well, with God's blessing, you too shall be changed into dearest friends."[40]

Elizabeth's talents and wealth of experience would be transformed through God's plan for her life. Even some family members and friends who had turned against her became impressed by Elizabeth's ability to forgive and help those who had hurt her. Elizabeth's wisdom is reflected in her words, "The Judge [who] will show Mercy in proportion to what we show."[41] Her compassion is revealed by her heart, which was not afraid to love. "Our Adored gave us a heart to love each other without restraints, calculations, or fears of saying too much or too little."[42]

All through her life, she fought for what she believed in, trusted in God's defense, and turned dreams into reality. She was a true daughter of the American Revolution who brought freedom for others. Because of her pioneering work, people could choose an affordable Catholic education and have access to the social services her religious sisters provided. They were offered opportunities which resulted from education and from the care that alleviates suffering and restores dignity.

CHAPTER SEVEN

· · · · · · · · · · · ·

The Spirit of Love and Service

"Perseverance is a great grace—to go on gaining and advancing every day, we must be resolute, and bear and suffer what our blessed forerunners did."[1]

On September, 11, 1975, a Joint Resolution of the 94th Congress of the United States of America was approved. It declared that Elizabeth Seton "will be canonized and proclaimed to be a saint on September 14, 1975, at official ceremonies in Saint Peter's Basilica in Rome, thus becoming the first person born in what is now the United States to be so recognized."[2]

It further stated that:

Whereas Elizabeth Seton, who will then be known as Saint Elizabeth Seton, through her own life and work and through the work of thousands of women who traced the origins of their religious foundations to her founding of the Sisters of Charity of Saint Joseph of Emmitsburg,

Maryland, on July 31, 1809, made an extraordinary contri-
bution to the religious and moral life of our country as well
as to the education, health, and welfare of vast numbers of
our citizens.[3]

When the Catholic Church canonized Elizabeth Ann Seton
on September 14, 1975, citizens in the United States celebrated
"National Saint Elizabeth Seton Day."[4] The American flag flown
over the Capitol building in Washington, D.C., on that date is
currently in her house on Paca Street in Baltimore. Later, in
2006, she was declared a patroness of Maryland.

A little over a quarter of a century later, the United States
was attacked by terrorists. The former World Trade Center
Towers once stood across the street from the churches where
Elizabeth worshiped as an Episcopalian at Saint Paul's and as a
Catholic at Saint Peter's. On September 14, 2001, President
George W. Bush declared a day of prayer and remembrance for
the victims of 9/11 and our nation. Even without electrical
power, the bell at Saint Paul's Church rang that day. It was the
twenty-sixth canonization anniversary of our nation's first native-
born saint. In the Catholic Church, it was also the feast day of
the Triumph of the Cross.

The cross marked the life of Elizabeth Ann Seton whose story
is a fully American story. In 1817, she wrote "This is not a country . . . for Solitude and Silence, but of warfare and crucifixion."[5]
She had already lived through the Revolutionary War in New
York and the War of 1812 in Maryland. Her life was a story of
confrontation and initiative. In order to succeed, she put aside
fear and sought God's help and support in fighting her battles.
Her assurance was faith. "Religion alone can bind that cord over

which neither circumstances, time, or Death can have no power. . . . For our Blessed Saviour Sanctifies and approves in US all the endearing ties and connections of our existence."[6] Elizabeth saw the events of her life from the perspective of eternity.

She also had a global view of existence. Toward the beginning of her time in Emmitsburg, she wrote about her work with the community of sisters. "Every corner of the world is the same to me if I may but serve our Lord."[7] She expressed her worldview to her son, William, when the War of 1812 ended. "Your poor Mother looks only at Souls. I see neither American nor English, but Souls redeemed, and lost. But you must, your case is quite different, love your country, yet also all countries, my William, see things as they are. Passions and excesses you will find everywhere."[8]

---·•·---

God works through the helping hands of people who are often strangers. Their skills and abilities are instruments of the Good Shepherd. Some perform heroic deeds and others simply offer kind words. No matter how small the action, it is the gesture of the heart that matters.

Elizabeth Seton's Sisters and Daughters of Charity have helped ease the suffering of soldiers in the aftermath of Civil War battles as well as twenty-first-century 9/11 victims in the dust-clogged streets of Lower Manhattan. Elizabeth's example, mission, and legacy have motivated women and men to serve the poor in mind, body, and spirit.

The four churches in Lower Manhattan associated with Elizabeth remained intact and played a part in the relief efforts following the tragic attacks. Saint Peter's Catholic Church, where Elizabeth made her profession of faith and received her First Holy Communion, stored food for the firefighters and the rescue dogs. Father Mychal Judge, OFM, a chaplain with the New York City Fire Department who died on 9/11, was brought there and laid by the altar. Father Judge had been educated by the Sisters of Charity of New York. The sisters continued to help the 9/11 victims and their families years after the tragedy.

On the night of September 10, homeless men who were sleeping in Saint Paul's Episcopal Church opened some windows to vent the hot, stuffy air. Thus, instead of shattering the windows, the rushing air from the towers' collapse went through the windows. Saint Paul's became a shelter for the weary rescue workers and a continuous source of food supplied by donors and served by volunteers. Others provided emotional and spiritual support for the workers. In 2004, a stunning exhibit opened at Saint Paul's: *Unwavering Spirit: Hope and Healing at Ground Zero* recounts the story of the rescue and recovery workers and volunteers.[9] At the Pilgrimage Altar, visitors from around the world have written hopeful and loving messages and left them for all to see. Today as you leave Saint Paul's, the new Freedom Tower rises to majestic heights and reflects the sunlight across lower Manhattan.

The site of Elizabeth's former home on State Street, Our Lady of the Rosary Catholic Church, also reached out to help. People stopped there to pray and asked for paper towels to wipe the dust from their faces. In her church, men and women began to piece together their dignity, which had been so roughly shattered on that cloudless September morning. Because of Elizabeth

Seton, who had suffered in mind, body, and spirit in that very place, others would now be comforted. Her church would later accommodate the Episcopalians from Trinity Church on Wall Street while that area recovered.

The connection between Our Lady of the Rosary Church and the Episcopal Trinity Church was made possible by the legacy of Elizabeth Seton. This relationship was named "Seton Bridge." In his sermon on September 16, 2001, the Reverend Samuel Johnson Howard of Trinity Church summed up the association this way, "We lived and worked in the shadow of the World Trade Center. Now we live and work in the shadow of the Cross."[10] He mentioned Elizabeth Seton.

> She was our daughter before she was their [the Catholics'] mother, and she is with us still today. . . . She furnishes an extraordinary link and it's that link, that bridge, that brings us to this shrine today and makes this, for at least a few moments, Trinity Church.[11]

————•————

Saint Elizabeth Ann Seton was declared the "Patroness of the Sea Services" in 1975, and therefore has a special connection to the United States Navy. During the Annual Sea Services Pilgrimage Mass at the shrine in Emmitsburg, Sea Services medals are blessed.[12] It also says, "May you have the special protection of this first American-born saint and mother throughout your Navy career."[13]

The Catholic Chapel in Bancroft Hall at the United States Naval Academy in Annapolis, Maryland, has a window dedicated to Elizabeth Seton. She is shown looking at a nineteenth-century ship, the *U.S.S. Cyane*, on which her son Richard served.

The fate of the Seton's shipping business demonstrated that merchant vessels need protection too. Elizabeth often used maritime images in her writing. She experienced terrifying storms during her sea voyages to Italy and to Baltimore. She knew what it was like to be in harm's way on the water. In the many letters she wrote to her sons, she revealed that she was concerned about their well-being and the safety of their souls as well.

Elizabeth exemplifies the virtues of courage, perseverance, and loyalty. As a daughter of the American Revolution and the Patroness of the United States Sea Services, she represents a woman who never gave up when faced with challenges. Today you can pray for her intercession anywhere and ask for her protection on the seas of your life.

CHAPTER EIGHT

• • • • • • • • • • • •

Divine Education

"Be but faithful to God with your whole heart, and never fear. He will support, direct, console, and finally crown your dearest Hope."[1]

Many people lead exemplary lives of faith, hope, and charity. But when the Catholic Church canonizes someone, it asks the question: Did this person practice the virtues of faith, hope, and charity to a heroic degree? Therefore, what matters most is how and why the person accomplished the work of his or her life.

Examples of heroism are constantly found on a battlefield. Many soldiers act courageously even when they might not feel brave. However, extraordinary, selfless acts of valor and risk are recognized by the military. It is the same with the saints. They have practiced faith, hope, and charity to the point of recognition in their Catholic communities. Their attitude in life magnified the wide spectrum of virtue.

——•◆•——

In order to understand Elizabeth's joyful approach to life, it helps to look at the connection between faith, hope, and charity. Elizabeth's life embraced those three theological virtues of the Christian Church. She needed faith in order to want to do God's will.

> Faith is the theological virtue by which we believe in God.... By faith "man freely commits his entire self to God." For this reason the believer seeks to know and do God's will. . . . Living faith "work[s] through charity." (*CCC*, no. 1814)

Elizabeth also needed a reason to motivate her to do God's will day in and day out, year after year, in good times and in suffering. That reason was hope for eternal life.

> Hope is the theological virtue by which we desire the kingdom of heaven and eternal life as our happiness, placing our trust in Christ's promises and relying not on our own strength, but on the help of the grace of the Holy Spirit. (*CCC*, no. 1817)

> It [hope] affords us joy even under trial. (*CCC*, no. 1820)

> We can therefore hope in the glory of heaven promised by God to those who love him and do his will. (*CCC*, no. 1821)

Thus, to do God's will obtains assurance for the eternal reward of heaven.

And finally, but most importantly, Elizabeth put her faith and hope into action by means of love or charity. That is why and how she turned the ordinary into the extraordinary. Her selfless-ness and love for others reflected the love of God. Her joyful spirit radiated the light and fire of God's love. "Charity is the theological virtue by which we love God above all things for his own sake, and our neighbor as ourselves for the love of God" (*CCC*, no. 1822).

The Apostle Paul writes that love "bears all things, believes all things, hopes all things, endures all things" (1 Cor 13:7). "And now faith, hope, and love abide, these three; and the greatest of these is love" (1 Cor 13:13).

———•◆•———

Charity is fueled by love and produces joy. Therefore, Elizabeth, as an instrument of God's love, received joy from each phase of her life. Joy is stronger than happiness, because it endures in good times and in bad. It bears fruit. Elizabeth did not gloss over hardships. On the contrary, she embraced hardships with common sense and a sense of purpose. She transformed suffering into joyful service with prayer. Faith assured her that in time God would enable all things to work out.

Even as a little girl, Elizabeth saw the bigger picture. She told her younger stepsister about God while she watched the sun set. She was comforted after the death of her own mother and sister with the knowledge that they were with God. She enjoyed her solitary walks, looking up at the clouds and absorbing the beauty of nature.[2]

During her teenage years, she missed her own father during his long absences from home. She grew to delight in the knowledge that God would always be her Father. Toward the end of her teenage years, family troubles beyond her control made Elizabeth miserable. Immersing herself in the society around her did not help. She preferred to be alone with God, and she imagined the day when she could live in the country and teach little children their prayers.[3]

As a debutante, she revealed her musical talent in her love for dancing. Joy was the music that kept her soul dancing during her entire life. Her popularity during the dances indicated that this lovely young woman must have smiled with the radiant joy that filled her heart and soul.

Elizabeth married for love and endured the pain of watching her husband's business and health decline. He was her soul-mate, and their marriage was a true partnership. William's fine character was evident in the respect that Elizabeth had for him. He was musical, worldly in a good sense, and he put her in a position to be well connected to the social and financial elite of New York. Although he could not ultimately provide for her, William's Italian friends and loyal connections in the United States would ensure the later success of her religious order.

When William shared the hardships of his family's business with Elizabeth, he also showed great confidence in and respect for her intelligence, management skills, and leadership abilities. Elizabeth's charitable work for the Society for the Relief of Poor Widows with Small Children demonstrated that she was not content to stay in the typical mold of a society woman of the late 1700s and early 1800s. Her charitable work connected her with the poor in an intimate way, and her selfless nature took root outside the comfort zones of her class. William admired and relied on her, which was a quiet source of joy. This mutual respect provided the climate where maturation and growth flourished.

In her marriage, Elizabeth was fully accepted, understood, and loved. William's love and support was her anchor and provided her with purpose. Her perseverance was his emotional nourishment and strength. Their relationship provided space where she could reach out to others and to God.

However, for anyone who thought the Setons' marriage was perfect, Elizabeth's views on marrying reveal that she was no stranger to marital stress. "The very best of these men (one is writing opposite to me [William]) are so unruly and perplexing that nothing should induce a reasonable Woman to wear the Chains of two of them, and that is the plain English of Matrimony."[4]

Motherhood was a great source of joy for Elizabeth. Nurturing and teaching came naturally to her. Blessed with five children of her own, she had the responsibility of bringing up William's step-siblings as well. William's younger step-sisters, Cecilia and Harriet, followed Elizabeth's example and converted to Catholicism. They remained close to Elizabeth in life and in death. Her soul-sister and step-sister, Rebecca, died in New York shortly after Elizabeth arrived home from Italy. These friendships were centered on God. Perhaps she thought of them when she said, "God is like a looking glass in which souls see each other."[5]

Before she left for Italy in 1803, Elizabeth had packed up and said good-bye to many of her possessions, to compensate for William Seton's debts. Instead of mourning her separation from these items, she embraced the loss.[6] By lightening the material load, she had more room for the spiritual.

After her husband's death in Italy, Elizabeth experienced the delight of discovery in the Catholic faith. She enjoyed touring the beautiful churches in Tuscany and learning about the saints, and she formed a new bond with Mary, the Mother of Jesus. Deprived of a mother's love so early in her life, Elizabeth now welcomed the maternal comfort of her Mother in Heaven.

Conversion to Catholicism brought her the greatest joy in life when she received the Eucharist for the first time. She referred to it as the "Supreme happiness it [her heart] had so long desired."[7] The bleak days of poverty in New York continued, but she now had this presence of God within her to fortify her spirit.

Her joyous arrival at Saint Mary's Seminary in Catholic Baltimore was an answer to prayer. Her vocation took shape there; then she traveled to Emmitsburg to fulfill her mission in life. Elizabeth lived with her students in Baltimore and Emmitsburg. In 1810, she wrote that she was "at Peace . . . in the midst of fifty children."[8] "I am as a Mother encompassed by many children of different dispositions . . . bound to love, instruct, and provide for the happiness of all, to give the example of cheerfulness."[9] Elizabeth treated each child as a child of God, and she did not discriminate based on behavior or social status. Her teenaged desire of living in the country and teaching children their prayers became reality in Maryland.

Elizabeth's ability to lead the Sisters of Charity is reflected in her joy of service. ". . . To speak the joy of my soul at the prospect of being able to assist the Poor, visit the sick, comfort the sorrowful, clothe little innocents, and teach them to love God!"[10]

Her principles and the ability to stick to them gave her peace of mind. "The first Rule of Christian charity—to believe no ill if we have not seen it; and to be silent, if we have seen it."[11] As Elizabeth's earthly life came to a close, her cheerful heart longed for the day when it would be united with God, the source of all her love and her joy.

——•◆•——

Elizabeth was a witness and servant of the Gospel of Christ. She listened to God in her prayer and also recognized when God spoke to her through other people. For example, she was a recipient of charity after her husband's death. When people reached out to her, she realized God was providing for her and her children. Her gratitude always included God. Her story was not the usual American dream of rags to riches. Elizabeth went from riches to rags to enrich the lives of others.

Works of mercy are described in Matthew's Gospel. Jesus points out that he is present in the poor and needy (see Mt 25:31–46). The corporal works of mercy are to feed the hungry, give drink to the thirsty, clothe the naked, shelter the homeless, visit the sick, visit the imprisoned, and bury the dead (see *CCC*, no. 2447). Just as people have throughout time, Elizabeth did all these things by caring for her family. In the *lazaretto* in Livorno, she suffered imprisonment. When the Filicchis visited the *lazaretto*, she knew what it was like to be visited in prison. Through her work with the Society for the Relief of Poor Widows with Small Children, the schools in Baltimore and Emmitsburg, and her Sisters of Charity, Elizabeth continued to perform corporal works of mercy.

The spiritual works of mercy are to instruct the ignorant, counsel the doubtful, admonish sinners, bear wrongs patiently, forgive offenses willingly, comfort the afflicted, and pray for the living and the dead (see *CCC*, no. 2447). Beginning with her own family, within the structure of the domestic church, Elizabeth practiced all these works throughout the stages of her life.

Her spiritual directors helped guide and teach her. But it was God, through his word in the Bible, who provided her with daily instruction. Elizabeth was always eager to learn. Her spiritual hunger was never satiated on earth. In the Sermon on the Mount, Jesus said that God will reward such a hunger in heaven. "Blessed are those who hunger and thirst for righteousness, for they will be filled" (Mt 5:6).

How did Elizabeth accomplish her goals?

She said: "Let your chief study be to acquaint yourself with God because there is nothing greater than God, and because it is the only knowledge which can fill the Heart with a Peace and joy, which nothing can disturb."[12]

She also disciplined herself. In today's world of internet distractions, her advice still applies: "Curiosity . . . which keeps us engaged in what is [going on], brings home many a foolish companion for our thoughts, to break the silence and peace our Lord desires to find in us."[13]

By reflecting God's love with fortitude, charity, and gratitude, she changed "Why, God?" into "Why not?" Her response to hardship was to share her time, gifts, and talents with others even if it meant self-denial, risk, and poverty. Her dreams became real by serving God and others. Lives were changed.

Acts of charity also gave Elizabeth freedom. As long as she served God, she was not weighed down by what others thought about her. She was free to take risks and to risk love. She did not let ill health, her past, hurt feelings, or daily hardships disconnect her from God in the present. In her words, "Who can bind the Soul which God sets free!"[14]

In order to do the work of God, we need tools. Elizabeth, the educator, offered some suggestions. She mentioned "good reading, prayer, the Sacraments . . . good resolutions often renewed."[15] She advised doing devotional reading every day[16] and to

> pray literally without ceasing . . . in every occurrence and employment of our lives. You know, I mean that prayer of the heart, which is independent of place or situation, or which is rather a habit of lifting up the heart to God as in a constant communication with Him.[17]

Elizabeth cautioned people not to judge others, because it was possible to misunderstand what motivates their actions.[18] She had faced judgment during her process of conversion to Catholicism, and she saw the better, far-reaching value of being fair. By pointing out the good in others who were being judged, she encouraged others to do the same. Her concern was "peace of conscience."[19] Elizabeth examined her conscience, acknowledged her sins, sought God's forgiveness, forgave others, and moved on. Only God's judgment mattered in the long run.

———•———

Today, as the ferry pulls away from the dock at the lower tip of Manhattan, you can imagine Elizabeth standing in front of her State Street house at the water's edge and searching the sky for the one who loves her best. Her former home harbors the past and her saintly story. In the present landscape, sea and sky converge at the tip of the island with a feeling of eternal promise.

The Manhattan skyline has changed repeatedly since Elizabeth lived on State Street. But her example remains the same, for God is reliable and constant. Elizabeth survived the storms of her life, and the church dedicated to her has survived storms—for example Hurricane Sandy and the terrorist attacks of 9/11. If her association with this State Street site has helped to preserve its place at the edge of Manhattan for centuries, it is possible for her legacy to help you now as well.

In 1808, Elizabeth sailed slowly out of New York harbor on a ship bound for Baltimore. She looked back at New York for the very last time and wrote about her house.

> I saw once more the windows of State Street—Oh my Lord in that hour—can a heart swell so high and not burst?
>
> Think of me when you pass it again—battering the waves of my changeable life—yet would I change one shade or trial of it—that would be madness.
>
> Oh no, the dear dear dear Adored Will be done through every moment of it, may it control, regulate and perfect us.
>
> And when all is over, how we will rejoice.[20]

Elizabeth was right. Her spirit of joy lives on in her legacy. The works of her generous, cheerful heart continue. Those who enter her Baltimore house today see a plaque with excerpts from the canonization homily of Pope Paul VI:

> Rejoice, we say to the great nation of the United States of America. Rejoice for your glorious daughter. Be proud of her. . . . May the dynamism and authenticity of her life be an example in our day—and for generations to come.[21]

Amen. Saint Elizabeth Ann Seton, pray for us and for the United States of America.

· · · · · · · · · · · ·

Prayer in Honor of
Saint Elizabeth Ann Seton

Lord God, thank you for blessing
Saint Elizabeth Ann Seton with great faith, hope, joy,
    and charity.
I pray that her timeless example will guide me.
I look at her humility to help me accept your will
    for my life.
Let her grateful heart remind me to thank you
for the joys and challenges of life.
May her courage and perseverance inspire me
to serve others, our church, and our country.
Thank you, God, for Elizabeth Seton,
a loving and glorious saint who is always by our side.
Elizabeth Ann Seton, pray for me! Amen.

. . . .

Reflection Questions

1. If you love and respect someone, you try to spend time getting to know the person. It may be an effort to communicate with your friend if the person doesn't live close by, but it is worth it. How do you communicate with a saint? You could read what the saint wrote and what was written about him or her. If possible, you can visit places connected with the saint. Meeting other people who share your interest and love for a saint is a delightful experience. Try it. And of course you can pray and ask for that saint's intercession. How can you learn more about the saints? Which saints do you feel drawn to?

2. Whom do you look up to? Perhaps they are wise family members or patient friends. What about secular "saints"? Today's culture constantly offers photos and

information about celebrities and athletes. You may admire them, dress like them, follow their daily lives, and buy their products. In her day, Elizabeth would have been a social celebrity.

People don't usually dress like the saints, but we admire and honor them. We can also pray for their intercession to God in heaven. Because prayer connects us to God and the saints, we can form friendships with them. On her own spiritual journey, Elizabeth was influenced by the saints. Like them, she fulfilled her Christian vocation and so she can offer a proven way for today's challenges.

Whom do you admire? How do they live their lives? How have they helped you to live your life?

3. The many dimensions of human experiences connect saints to people in any time or place. Elizabeth experienced a wide range of challenges and joys as a daughter, wife, mother, laborer, and convert to Catholicism. God's love and the hope for eternal life gave purpose, meaning, and direction to Elizabeth's life. Elizabeth's sacrifice and service to others gave her peace. That peace of God is also meant for us. She changed "Why, God?" into "With God's help, why not?"

How might Elizabeth's life resonate with your own experience? Have you ever asked, "Why, God?" How might God be calling you to deeper trust in his wisdom and providence?

4. The Seton family motto, "Hazard yet forward," speaks about going forward despite the risks. Elizabeth trusted God, and he helped her conquer natural fears and apprehensions while she carried life's crosses. Without excessive, self-defeating mental baggage, she was able to make decisions and plans with a clear, open mind and unencumbered heart. She saw possibilities, not inevitabilities.

How can Elizabeth's example help you face change? Think of an example from Elizabeth's life that could reveal a new way to look at the challenge of change in your life.

5. The name "Elizabeth" reminds us of a great friendship described in the Visitation, the second joyful mystery of the Rosary. After the angel Gabriel appeared to Mary, she went to visit her older cousin, Elizabeth. Elizabeth greeted Mary with these words, *"Blessed are you among women, and blessed is the fruit of your womb"* (Lk 1:42). These two holy women, separated by age and distance, shared the common bond of faith, friendship, and expectant motherhood.

Elizabeth Seton is a little like Mary's cousin, Elizabeth. As a saint, Elizabeth Seton knows the depths of your soul when you come to her in prayer. She shares your concerns and you go away enriched by her example and intercession in heaven.

Elizabeth's middle name, Ann, is the name of the Virgin Mary's mother. She gave Mary life and helped guide her to become the holiest of women. Like Saint Anne, Saint Elizabeth Ann Seton is a role model for mothers. She can nurture your faith by her example.

Think about these holy women: Saint Elizabeth, Saint Anne, and Saint Elizabeth Ann Seton. Do you have friends who demonstrate the qualities found in these saints? How have these friends influenced your life?

6. Elizabeth did not consult God only once in a while when she felt like it. Instead, she tried to seek his guidance in her daily life. She submitted her will to his will in order for him to use the gifts and talents she knew she had, and also the ones she didn't know she had. God brought out the best in her, and he can do this for everyone.

    God uses the people around you and your current circumstances to give you experiences that can help prepare you for the future. Think about Elizabeth's humility and how she trusted in God. How can you use Elizabeth's example to help you trust God and to find his plan for your daily life?

7. Elizabeth understood the importance of self-knowledge in her relationship with God. She developed her gifts and talents to be the person God created her to be.

    Whether she was rich or poor, Episcopalian or Catholic, her identity was focused on God, who gave her confidence. How can you use Elizabeth's example of self-knowledge in your life?

8. Learning about a saint can take a lifetime. Use the references and websites at the end of this book to continue your journey with Elizabeth.

How does this verse from Psalm 86 remind you of Elizabeth's journey with God?

"Teach me your way, O LORD,
that I may walk in your truth;
give me an undivided heart
to revere your name.
I give thanks to you, O LORD my God, with my
    whole heart,
. . . and I will glorify your name forever." (Ps 86:12)

Chronology

August 28, 1774—Elizabeth Ann Bayley was born in the area of New York City.

1777—Catherine Bayley, Elizabeth's mother, dies.

January 25, 1794—Elizabeth Bayley marries William Magee Seton in New York City.

May 3, 1795—Elizabeth gives birth to Anna Maria Seton.

November 25, 1796—Elizabeth gives birth to William M. Seton.

January 1798—Financial problems for Seton, Maitland, and Company begin.

July 20, 1798—Elizabeth gives birth to Richard Bayley Seton.

June 28, 1800—Elizabeth gives birth to Catherine Charlton Seton.

August 17, 1801—Dr. Richard Bayley, Elizabeth's father, dies.

August 20, 1802—Elizabeth gives birth to Rebecca Mary Seton.

October 2, 1803—Elizabeth, William, and Anna Seton travel to Livorno, Italy.

December 27, 1803—William Magee Seton dies in Pisa, Italy.

June 4, 1804—Elizabeth and Anna returned to New York.

March 14, 1805—Elizabeth is received into the Catholic Church at Saint Peter's in New York City.

March 25, 1805—Elizabeth experiences her First Holy Communion at Saint Peter's Church.

May 25, 1806—Elizabeth's has her Confirmation at Saint Peter's Church.

June 9–June 15, 1808—The Seton family travels from New York to Baltimore.

June 16, 1808—The Seton family arrives at Saint Mary's Seminary in Baltimore.

Summer/Fall of 1808—Elizabeth opens her school for girls.

March 25, 1809—Elizabeth pronounces private vows in the lower chapel at Saint Mary's and Bishop John Carroll calls her Mother Seton for the first time.

June 9, 1809—Mother Seton and her religious sisters first appear in the habit of the Sisters of Charity.

June 1809—The group travels to Emmitsburg, Maryland.

July 31, 1809—Sisters of Charity of Saint Joseph's in Emmitsburg, Maryland is founded.

February 1810—Saint Joseph's Free School opens in Emmitsburg.

May 1810—Saint Joseph's Academy is established in Emmitsburg.

January 17, 1812—The *Regulations of the Sisters of Charity in the United States of America*, based on the Rules of the Daughters of Charity (founded in France in 1633) are confirmed.

March 12, 1812—Anna Maria Seton dies.

July 19, 1813—Religious sisters pronounce their first vows as Sisters of Charity of Saint Joseph's.

November 3, 1816—Rebecca Mary Seton dies.

January 4, 1821—Elizabeth Ann Seton dies. Her relics are entombed in the Altar of Relics in the Basilica at the National Shrine of Saint Elizabeth Ann Seton in Emmitsburg, Maryland.[1]

June 26, 1823—Richard Bayley Seton dies.

January 13, 1868—William M. Seton dies.

April 3, 1891—Catherine Charlton Seton (Mother Mary Catherine) dies.

October 1907—Informative Cause of Process for Canonization is begun by James Cardinal Gibbons.

December 18, 1959—Pope John XXIII proclaims Mother Seton venerable.

March 17, 1963—Pope John XXIII proclaims Elizabeth Ann Seton blessed.

September 14, 1975—Pope Paul VI canonizes Saint Elizabeth Ann Seton.

1975—Mother Seton named Patroness of the United States Sea Services.

2006—Mother Seton becomes a Patroness of the State of Maryland.

· · · · · · · · · · · ·

Bibliography and Sources

THE WRITINGS OF SAINT ELIZABETH ANN SETON

Seton, Elizabeth Bayley. *Elizabeth Bayley Seton: A Woman of Prayer*. Edited by Sister Marie Celeste, S.C. Staten Island, New York: Alba House, 1993.

———. *Elizabeth Bayley Seton Collected Writings*, Volumes 1, 2, 3a, and 3b. Edited by Regina Bechtle, S.C., and Judith Metz, S.C. Manuscript editor Ellin M. Kelly. Hyde Park, New York: New City Press, 2000–2006.

———. *Friendship of My Soul, Selected Letters by Elizabeth Ann Seton, 1803–1809*. Compiled and edited by Betty Ann Mc-Neil, D.C. Emmitsburg, Maryland: Daughters of Charity of Saint Vincent de Paul, 2010.

———. *Light and Grace: Elizabeth Seton on Life, Faith, and Eternity*. Edited by Betty Ann McNeil, D.C. Emmitsburg, Maryland: The National Shrine of Saint Elizabeth Ann Seton. [No date.] Writings selected from *Elizabeth Bayley Seton Collected Writings*, Regina Bechtle, S.C., and Judith Metz., S.C., eds., Ellin M. Kelly, mss.ed., 3 vols. New York: New City Press, 2000–2006.

———. *Numerous Choirs: A Chronicle of Elizabeth Bayley Seton and Her Spiritual Daughters, Volume I: The Seton Years, 1774–1821.* Compiled and edited by Ellin M. Kelly. Evansville, Indiana: Mater Dei Provincialate, 1981.

BOOKS

Alderman, Margaret, and Josephine Burns, D.C. *Praying with Elizabeth Seton*. Winona, Minnesota: Saint Mary's Press, Christian Brothers Publications, 1992.

Book of Common Prayer, and Administration of the Sacraments, and Other Rites and Ceremonies of the Church, According to the Use of the Protestant Episcopal Church in the United States of America. Philadelphia: S. Potter & Co., 1818. *By the Bishops, the Clergy, and the Laity of the Protestant Episcopal Church in the United States of America, in Convention, October 16, 1789. This Book shall be in use from and after October 1, 1790.*

Burns, Ric, and James Sanders. *New York: An Illustrated History*, Expanded edition. New York: Alfred A. Knopf, 2008.

Catechism of the Catholic Church. 2nd ed. Washington, DC: Libreria Editrice Vaticana, 1994.

de Chantal, Jane Frances. *A Simple Life, Wisdom from Jane Frances de Chantal*. Edited by Kathryn Hermes, FSP. Boston: Pauline Books & Media, 2011.

Dirvin, Joseph I., C.M. *The Soul of Elizabeth Seton*. San Francisco: Ignatius Press, 1990.

Dirvin, Joseph I., C.M. *Mrs. Seton, Foundress of the American Sisters of Charity*. Emmitsburg, Maryland: Basilica of the National Shrine of St. Elizabeth Ann Seton, 1993.

Fugazy, M. Irene, SC. *Elizabeth Ann Seton*. Rome: Editions du Signe, 1997.

Heidish, Marcy. *Defiant Daughters: Christian Women of Conscience*. Liguori, Missouri: Liguori Publications, 2010.

Holy Bible, New Revised Standard Version, Catholic Edition. Nashville, Tennessee: Division of Christian Education of the National Council of the Churches of Christ, 1993.

Johnson, Samuel. *The Rambler*. London: J. M. Dent & Sons Ltd., 1963.

Lamb, Martha J. *History of the City of New York*, Volume II. New York: A. S. Barnes and Company, 1880.

Martin, James, SJ. *My Life with the Saints*. Chicago: Loyola Press, 2006.

McCullough, David. *1776*. New York: Simon & Schuster, 2005.

McNeil, Betty Ann, D.C. *15 Days of Prayer with Saint Elizabeth Ann Seton*. Liguori, Missouri: Liguori Publications, 2002.

_____. *The Mountain and the Valley of Saint Elizabeth Ann Seton at Emmitsburg*. Emmitsburg, Maryland: Sisters of Charity of Saint Joseph's, Inc., 2009.

Melville, Annabelle M. *Elizabeth Bayley Seton, 1774–1821*. Edited by Betty Ann McNeil, D.C. Hanover, Pennsylvania: The Sheridan Press, 2009.

Merton, Thomas. *The Seven Storey Mountain*. Fiftieth Anniversary Edition. New York: Harcourt Brace & Company, (1948), 1998.

Metz, Judith, S.C. *A Retreat with Elizabeth Seton, Meeting Our Grace*. Mount St. Joseph, Ohio: Sisters of Charity of Cincinnati, 2011.

Thoreau, Henry David. *Walden and Civil Disobedience*. New York: Penguin Classics, 1986.

Walters, Julie. *Elizabeth Ann Seton, Saint for a New Nation*. Mahwah, New Jersey: Paulist Press, 2002.

NEWSLETTERS

The Seton Way, Vol. 10, No. 1. Emmitsburg, Maryland: National Shrine of Saint Elizabeth Ann Seton, Winter 2001.

Trinity News, Vol. 48, No. 1. New York: The Parish of Trinity Church in the City of New York, Fall 2001.

Pilgrimage Sites

Basilica of the National Shrine
    of the Immaculate Conception
400 Michigan Avenue, NE
Washington, DC 20017–1566
www.nationalshrine.com

The Mother Seton House and
Old Saint Mary's Seminary Chapel
Saint Mary's Spiritual Center and Historic Site
600 North Paca Street, Baltimore, Maryland 21201
www.stmarysspiritualcenter.org

The National Shrine of Saint Elizabeth Ann Seton
339 South Seton Avenue
Emmitsburg, Maryland 21727
www.setonheritage.org

Parrocchia Madre Seton
(Church of Saint Elizabeth Ann Seton)
Piazza M. Lavagna, 15, Livorno, Italy, 57125
www.madreseton.it

Saint Paul's Chapel
209 Broadway at Vesey Street
New York, NY 10007
www.saintpaulschapel.org

Saint Peter's Church
22 Barclay Street
New York, NY 10007
www.stpetersrcnyc.org

Shrine of Saint Elizabeth Ann Seton
Church of Our Lady of the Rosary
7 State Street, New York, NY 10004
www.setonshrine.com

Trinity Church
74 Trinity Place
Broadway at Wall Street
New York, NY 10006
www.trinitywallstreet.org

. . . .

Notes

DEDICATION

1. Regina Bechtle, S.C., and Judith Metz., S.C., eds., Ellin M. Kelly, mss. ed., *Elizabeth Bayley Seton Collected Writings*, 3 vols. (New City Press: New York, 2000–2006). [Hereinafter cited as CW with volume number and page number.] To Cecilia Seton, July 1, 1807, *CW*, 1: 466.

2. In a letter from George Washington to Phillip Schuyler, August 20, 1775.

INTRODUCTION

1. Associate Orientation Materials [unpublished, 1998], Sisters of Charity of New York, 31.

2. In quoting Elizabeth, the author has taken the liberty, on occasion, to correct and update her spelling and punctuation for the present-day reader.

3. Jane Frances de Chantal, *A Simple Life: Wisdom from Jane Frances de Chantal*, ed. Kathryn Hermes, FSP (Boston: Pauline Books & Media, 2011), xi.

Chapter One

1. Copy to Catherine Seton, July 4, 1820, *CW*, 2:660.

2. See Ric Burns and James Sanders, *New York: An Illustrated History*, Expanded edition,(Reprint, New York: Alfred A. Knopf, 2008), 30.

3. See Annabelle M. Melvile, *Elizabeth Bayley Seton, 1774–1821*, ed. Betty Ann McNeil, D.C. (Hanover, Pennsylvania: The Sheridan Press, 2009), 3. [Hereinafter cited in text as *Elizabeth Bayley Seton*.]

4. See *Elizabeth Bayley Seton*, 5.

5. Journal to Rebecca Seton, December 1, 1803, *CW*, 1:264.

6. See To Julia Scott, October 23, 1810, *CW*, 2:161.

Chapter Two

1. To Eliza Sadler, March 27, 1798, *CW*, 1:21.

2. See *Elizabeth Bayley Seton*, 21.

3. See ibid., 23.

4. See ibid.

5. See ibid., 16.

6. See Mrs. Martha J. Lamb, *History of the City of New York*, Vol. II (New York: A. S. Barnes & Co., 1880), 304. [Hereinafter cited in text as *History of the City of New York*, Vol. II.]

7. See *Elizabeth Bayley Seton*, 7 and 25.

8. *History of the City of New York*, Vol. II, 433.

9. Dear Remembrances, *CW*, 3a:513.

10. To William Seton, April 4, 1817, *CW*, 2:473.

11. To Julia Scott, December 1, 1814, *CW*, 2:287.

12. The Following of Christ, *CW* 3b:84.

13. Ibid.

14. To Eliza Sadler, August 1, 1797, *CW*, 1:17.

15. *The Book of Common Prayer, Protestant Episcopal Church in the United States of America* (Philadelphia: S. Potter & Co., 1818), 144. [Hereinafter cited in text as *The Book of Common Prayer*.]

16. To Rebecca Seton, December 23, 1799, *CW*, 1:107.

17. To Julia Scott, November 16, 1802, *CW*, 1:212.

18. Archives Province of St. Louise (APSL) 1–3-3–4 #119, from Cecilia O'Conway, Christmas 1818. Permission from Daughters of Charity Province of St. Louise Archives, Emmitsburg, Maryland.

19. To Julia Scott, December 19, 1798, *CW*, 1:55.

20. Ibid., July 5, 1798, *CW*, 1:35.

21. Ibid., November 19, 1800, *CW*, 1:140.

22. Ibid., December 26, 1800, *CW*, 1:143.

23. See *Elizabeth Bayley Seton*, 43.

24. See *Elizabeth Bayley Seton*, 74.

25. To Eliza Sadler, September 28, 1803, *CW*, 1:221.

26. Ibid., probably September 20, 1803, *CW*, 1:220.

27. Ibid., September 28, 1803, *CW*, 1:222.

28. To Julia Scott, October 1, 1803, *CW*, 1:222.

29. To Antonio Filicchi, May 6, 1805, *CW*, 1:362.

30. To Julia Scott, October 28, 1798, *CW*, 1:49.

31. Ibid., November 3, 1798, *CW*, 1:52.

CHAPTER THREE

1. To Antonio Filicchi, August 10, 1806, *CW*, 1:414.

2. To Julia Scott, October 28, 1803, *CW*, 1:245.

3. Journal to Rebecca Seton, November 8, 1803 in Gibraltar Bay, *CW*, 1:246.

4. See ibid., November 19, 1803, *CW*, 1:253.

5. Ibid., November 24, 1803, *CW*, 1:258.

6. See Ibid., November 20, 1803, *CW*, 1:254.

7. Ibid., November 24, 1803, *CW*, 1:257.

8. See ibid., December 12, 1803, *CW*, 1:268.

9. Ibid., November 25, 1803, *CW*, 1:259.

10. Ibid., December 13, 1803, *CW*, 1:269.

11. Ibid., December 13, 1803, *CW*, 1:269.

12. Ibid., *CW*, 1:270.

13. Journal to Rebecca Seton, December 24 (Saturday), 1803, *CW*, 1:273.

14. Ibid., December 1, 1803, *CW*, 1:265.

15. Ibid.

16. Ibid., November 19, 1803, *CW*, 1:252.

17. Ibid., November 29, 1803, *CW*, 1:261.

18. Ibid., November 30, 1803, *CW*, 1:261.

19. See ibid.

20. Ibid., quoted by Saint Elizabeth Ann Seton.

21. Journal to Rebecca Seton, December 26, 1803, *CW*, 1:274.

22. Ibid. (December 27, 1803).

23. Ibid.

24. See ibid., January 28, 1804, *CW*, 1:289.

25. Ibid.

26. See *Elizabeth Bayley Seton*, 96.

27. See To Rebecca Seton, February 24, 1804, *CW*, 1:293.

28. See Betty Ann McNeil, D.C., *The Mountain and the Valley of Saint Elizabeth Ann Seton at Emmitsburg* (Emmitsburg, Maryland: Sisters of Charity of St. Joseph's, Inc., 2009), 21. Also see Life of Louise de Marillac, *CW, 3b:355,* footnotes.

29. See *Elizabeth Bayley Seton*, 97.

30. To Rebecca Seton, February 10, 1804, *CW*, 1:291.

31. See ibid.

32. See *Elizabeth Bayley Seton*, 98.

33. Journal to Rebecca Seton continued, April 18, 1804, *CW*, 1:299.

CHAPTER FOUR

1. The Following of Christ, *CW*, 3b:79.

2. To Julia Scott. July 15, 1804, *CW*, 1:313.

3. Ibid.

4. To Antonio Filicchi, December 13, 1804, *CW*, 1:338.

5. Draft to Rev. John Henry Hobart, written at sea, undated, *CW*, 1:305.

6. Journal to Amabilia Filicchi, July 19, 1804, entry January 1805, *CW*, 1:373.

7. See Robert Seton Family Papers, University of Notre Dame Archives.

Simon Brute to William Seton, June 29, 1821. See also Account by Rev. Simon Brute, S. S., of Elizabeth Seton's Last Days, January 4, 1821, *CW*, 2:769.

8. Robert Seton Family Papers, University of Notre Dame Archives.

Simon Brute to William Seton, June 29, 1821.

9. Journal to Amabilia Filicchi, September 1804, *CW*, 1:370.

10. Ibid., January 1805 [entry March 20, 1805], *CW*, 1:376.

11. Draft to Mrs. William Raborg, June 1817, *CW*, 2:488.

12. Ibid., 488 and 489.

13. To Filippo Filicchi, November 2, 1807, *CW*, 1:480.

14. Journal to Amabilia Filicchi, March 25, 1805, *CW*, 1:376.

15. Ibid., *CW*, 1:377.

16. Ibid.

17. See Journal to Amabilia Filicchi, January 1805, *CW*, 1:374.

18. To Amabilia Filicchi, April 15, 1805, *CW*, 1:353.

19. See To Julia Scott, July 15, 1804, *CW*, 1:314.

20. See Journal to Amabilia Filicchi, August 28, 1804, *CW*, 1:369.

21. "Departed St. Teresa's Day," ASSUMPTION 1813 Mt. St. Mary, conclusion, *CW*, 3b:20.

22. See To Julia Scott, August 28, 1805, *CW*, 1:384.

23. Spiritual Journal to Cecilia Seton, October 15, 1807, *CW*, 1:477.

24. To Julia Scott, November 10, 1806, *CW*, 1:418.

25. To Eliza Sadler, January 20, 1809, *CW*, 2:50.

26. See *Elizabeth Bayley Seton*, 147 and 148.

27. See To Julia Scott, August 4, 1807, *CW*, 1:452.

28. To Antonio Filicchi, July 8, 1808, *CW*, 2:18.

29. Ibid.

CHAPTER FIVE

1. Elizabeth Seton's Prayer book, *CW*, 3b:73.

2. Ellin M. Kelly, ed. and comp., *Numerous Choirs: A Chronicle of Elizabeth Bayley Seton and Her Spiritual Daughters,* Vol. I: *The Seton Years, 1774–1821* (Evansville, Indiana: Mater Dei Provincialate, 1981), 28 and 29. Permission from Daughters of Charity Province of St. Louise Archives, Emmitsburg, Maryland.

3. See *Elizabeth Bayley Seton*, 43.

4. See ibid., 177.

5. To Cecilia Seton, June 14, 1808, *CW*, 2:4.

6. Ibid., *CW*, 2:5.

7. To Cecilia Seton, June 16, 1808, *CW*, 2:7.

8. To Julia Scott, July 4, 1808, *CW*, 2:15.

9. Ibid.

10. To Catherine Dupleix, June 20, 1808, *CW*, 2:9.

11. To Julia Scott, October 10, 1808, *CW*, 2:37.

12. Copy to Antonio Filicchi, July 8, 1808, *CW*, 2:19.

13. Ibid.

14. To Julia Scott, July 4, 1808, *CW*, 2:13 and 14.

15. Ibid., April 25, 1808, *CW*, 1:506.

16. See ibid., July 4, 1808, *CW*, 2:15.

17. Ibid.

18. See *Elizabeth Bayley Seton*, 185.

19. To Cecilia Seton, October 6, 1808, *CW*, 2:34.

20. See Regulations For the Society of Sisters of Charity in the United States of America, Chapter 1, Of the Ends of their Society and of the Virtues peculiar to their State, Article 1, *CW*, 3b:500.

21. Elizabeth Seton's Prayer book, *CW*, 3b:76.

22. The Following of Christ, *CW*, 3b:77.

23. Elizabeth Seton's Prayer book, *CW*, 3b:75.

24. To Eliza Sadler, January 20, 1809, *CW*, 2:48.

25. To Filippo Filicchi, January 21, 1809, *CW*, 2:53.

26. See *Elizabeth Bayley Seton*, 201.

Chapter Six

1. To Catherine Dupleix, January 1816, *CW*, 2:366.

2. See *Elizabeth Bayley Seton*, 198 (footnote).

3. See To Rev. William Dubourg, S.S., June 21, 1809, *CW*, 2:73.

4. Ibid.

5. To Matthias O'Conway, June 25, 1809, *CW*, 2:75.

6. See *Elizabeth Bayley Seton*, 211.

7. To Julia Scott, October 29, 1812, *CW*, 2:232.

8. To a Sister on One of the Missions, after October 1814, *CW*, 2:701.

9. See *Elizabeth Bayley Seton*, 213.

10. See ibid., 283.

11. See *CW*, 2:245, footnote 2.

12. To Rev. Simon Brute, S.S., August 1, 1817, *CW*, 2:494.

13. To Julia Scott, July 20, 1810, *CW*, 2:146.

14. Ibid., March 26, 1810, *CW*, 2:117.

15. Copy to George Weis, July 30, 1812, *CW*, 2:224–225.

16. To William Seton, November 11, 1816, *CW*, 2:447.

17. See *Elizabeth Bayley Seton*, 330.

18. To William Seton, November 11, 1816, *CW*, 2:447.

19. See *Elizabeth Bayley Seton*, 403.

20. To Julia Scott, May 6, 1805, *CW*, 1:361.

21. See *Elizabeth Bayley Seton*, 276.

22. Copy to William Seton, January 1815, *CW*, 2:297.

23. Ibid.

24. Copy to William Seton, January, 1815, *CW*, 2:298.

25. See *Elizabeth Bayley Seton*, 369.

26. See ibid., 362.

27. To Rev. Simon Brute, S.S., undated, *CW*, 2:683.

28. Draft to Mrs. William Raborg, June 1817, *CW*, 2:489.

29. Mother Seton's last writings, *CW*, 3a:255.

30. Rev. Dubourg was her first superior, and Rev. Dubois was her third superior.

31. See *Elizabeth Bayley Seton*, 233.

32. See ibid., 239.

33. Rev. John David to Elizabeth Seton, Baltimore, 28 December 1809, AMSV (Archives Mount Saint Vincent) 115, 1, 18. Archives Sisters of Charity of New York.

34. See *Elizabeth Bayley Seton*, 399.

35. Elizabeth Seton's Prayer book [p. 249], *CW*, 3b:74.

36. Mother Seton's last writings, *CW*, 3a:257.

37. Account by Rev. Simon Brute, S.S., of Elizabeth Seton's Last Days, 2d January 1821, *CW,* 2:767.

38. See To Antonio Filicchi, December 13, 1804, *CW*, 1:338.

39. See Sister Eleanor Casey, D.C., *Livorno, Italy—First Parish Named after Mother Seton* (Emmitsburg, Maryland: National Shrine of Saint Elizabeth Ann Seton, *The Seton Way*, Winter 2001).

40. Journal to Rebecca Seton, June 4, 1804, *CW*, 1:308.

41. Principal impressions, August 28, 1814, *CW*, 3b:39.

42. To Catherine Dupleix, date outside February 4, 1811, *CW*, 2:171.

Chapter Seven

1. Mother Seton's last writings, *CW*, 3a:261.

2. Public Law 94–95—Sept. 11, 1975, 89 Stat. 477, http://www.gpo.gov/fdsys/pkg/STATUTE-89/pdf/STATUTE-89-Pg477.pdf.

3. Ibid.

4. Ibid.

5. To Sister Cecilia O'Conway, before August 13, 1817, *CW, 2:499.*

6. To Julia Scott, November 16, 1802, *CW, 1:212.*

7. To Archbishop John Carroll, January 25, 1810, *CW, 2:106.*

8. To William Seton, February 16, 1815, *CW, 2:306.*

9. See St. Paul's Chapel, http://www.saintpaulschapel.org.

10. "In the Shadow of the Cross," Trinity News, Vol. 48, No. 1. (New York, NY: The Parish of Trinity Church in the City of New York, Fall 2001), 12.

11. Ibid., 12 and 13.

12. From the Navy Medal Pamphlet, *Commemorating Elizabeth Ann Seton, 1774–1821, Sainted Mother of Two U.S. Navy Sons* (Emmitsburg, Maryland: National Shrine of Saint Elizabeth Ann Seton, n.d.).

13. Ibid.

CHAPTER EIGHT

1. To Eliza Farquhar, undated, *CW*, 1:539.

2. See Dear Remembrances, *CW*, 3a:510–511.

3. See ibid., *CW*, 3a:512.

4. To Julia Scott, December 20, 1799, *CW*, 1:105.

5. "Union in God" [n.d.], *CW*, 3b:42.

6. See Dear Remembrances, *CW*, 3a:514.

7. Ibid., *CW*, 3a:519.

8. To Eliza Sadler, Postmarked August 3, *CW*, 2:153.

9. Ibid., *CW*, 2:154.

10. To Julia Scott, March 23, 1809, *CW*, 2:62.

11. Catherine Seton's Little Red Book, *CW*, 3a:508.

12. To Cecilia Seton, November 19, 1802, *CW*, 1:214.

13. Mother Seton's last writings, *CW*, 3a:259.

14. To Cecilia Seton, July 1, 1807, *CW*, 1:446.

15. "Departed St. Teresa's day," *CW*, 3b:12.

16. See ibid., and To Anna Maria Seton, 1803, *CW*, 1:219.

17. To Cecilia Seton, October 7, 1805, *CW*, 1:389.

18. See To Julia Scott, April 16, 1798, *CW*, 1:22.

19. Catherine Seton's Little Red Book, *CW*, 3a:492.

20. To Eliza Sadler, January 20, 1809, *CW*, 2:50.

21. Canonization of Elisabeth Ann Seton, *Homily of the Holy Father Paul VI*, September 14, 1975, http://www.vatican.va/holy_father/paul_vi/homilies/1975/documents/hf_p-vi_hom_19750914_en.html.

CHRONOLOGY

1. See http://www.setonheritage.org/learn-and-explore/virtual-tour/altar-of-relics.

BOOKS & MEDIA

A mission of the Daughters of St. Paul

As apostles of Jesus Christ, evangelizing today's world:

We are CALLED to holiness
by God's living Word and Eucharist.

We COMMUNICATE the Gospel message
through our lives and through all
available forms of media.

We SERVE the Church
by responding to the hopes and needs
of all people with the Word of God,
in the spirit of St. Paul.

For more information visit our Web site:
www.pauline.org.

BOOKS & MEDIA

The Daughters of St. Paul operate book and media centers at the following addresses. Visit, call, or write the one nearest you today, or find us at www.pauline.org.

CALIFORNIA

3908 Sepulveda Blvd, Culver City, CA 90230 — 310-397-8676
935 Brewster Avenue, Redwood City, CA 94063 — 650-369-4230
5945 Balboa Avenue, San Diego, CA 92111 — 858-565-9181

FLORIDA

145 S.W. 107th Avenue, Miami, FL 33174 — 305-559-6715

HAWAII

1143 Bishop Street, Honolulu, HI 96813 — 808-521-2731

ILLINOIS

172 North Michigan Avenue, Chicago, IL 60601 — 312-346-4228

LOUISIANA

4403 Veterans Memorial Blvd, Metairie, LA 70006 — 504-887-7631

MASSACHUSETTS

885 Providence Hwy, Dedham, MA 02026 — 781-326-5385

MISSOURI

9804 Watson Road, St. Louis, MO 63126 — 314-965-3512

NEW YORK

64 W. 38th Street, New York, NY 10018 — 212-754-1110

SOUTH CAROLINA

243 King Street, Charleston, SC 29401 — 843-577-0175

TEXAS

Currently no book center; for parish exhibits or outreach evangelization, contact: 210–488–4123 or SanAntonio@paulinemedia.com

VIRGINIA

1025 King Street, Alexandria, VA 22314 — 703-549-3806

CANADA

3022 Dufferin Street, Toronto, ON M6B 3T5 — 416-781-9131